Bible Study for Beginners

Unlocking the Essentials with Beginner-Friendly and Easy-to-Understand Explanations

Welcome Aboard, Check Out This Limited-Time Free Bonus!

Ahoy, reader! Welcome to the Ahoy Publications family, and thanks for snagging a copy of this book! Since you've chosen to join us on this journey, we'd like to offer you something special.

Check out the link below for a FREE e-book filled with delightful facts about American History.

But that's not all - you'll also have access to our exclusive email list with even more free e-books and insider knowledge. Well, what are ye waiting for? Click the link below to join and set sail toward exciting adventures in American History.

<u>Access your bonus here</u>
<u>https://ahoypublications.com/</u>
<u>Or, Scan the QR code!</u>

Table of Contents

Introduction

What often attracts many people to the study of the Bible is a quest for answers to several unanswered questions, a thirst for knowledge, or simply a stumble-upon-by-chance kind of situation. However, regardless of the initial reason, they often arrive at the same conclusion: The Bible is a treasure trove. It is filled with timeless wisdom, practical lessons, and insightful stories applicable in all areas of life.

Simply reading it isn't always that easy, as people often give up as they find it too cumbersome to understand or comprehend. *Where to begin?* Seems to be a common question. Are you stuck wondering where to start your exploration of the Bible without feeling overwhelmed?

This book was written to erase that concern and to give you easy access to the treasures of the Bible. The Bible Study Guide for Beginners is more than just a book; it's a guide that holds your hand and helps you navigate the timeless stories and teachings within the pages of the Bible. It guides you through the revelations of many of the most important chapters – Genesis, Exodus, Psalms, Proverbs, Matthew, Romans, Hebrews, down to Revelation. This exploration is a marathon, not a sprint, so you are encouraged to enjoy each passage at your own pace. As much of an insightful read as the Bible is, this guide will make it just as enjoyable. See it as having a casual chat about the scriptures.

So, if you've always wanted to explore the Bible but felt unsure about where to begin, consider this book your friendly companion and guide. It promises to make your journey of the Bible less complicated and more enjoyable. A life-changing discovery awaits you on the other side!

Note: There are several versions of the Bible written at different times – but mainly with the aim of improving readability – NOT changing its content or meaning. This book will use different versions, including the King James Version, the NIV (New International Version), and the NKJV (the New King James Version).

Chapter 1: Genesis Unveiled

It has been said that there is no fixed way to go about the study of the Bible or in what order it should be read. This is indeed true, but a good suggestion would be to start from where it all began. *Genesis* is the first book of the Bible, which literally means "beginning." It is also in line with the Hebrew title, which was coined from the first three words in Genesis, "in the beginning," which is translated into Biblical Hebrew as *Bereshit*. In the pages of Genesis lies the beauty of the unique formation and creation of the world.

Genesis is the first book of the Bible.
https://www.pexels.com/photo/close-up-photo-of-Bible-4654082/

The Book of Genesis is one part of a five-book volume referred to as the *Pentateuch* (or the "Torah" by the Jews – which means "Law"). The Torah comprises Genesis and four other books, Exodus, Leviticus, Numbers, and Deuteronomy, which will be explored later. The deep history found in Genesis is interwoven with rich lessons that are applicable to one's life. The action of the stories in this book, from the Garden of Eden, the fall of man, to God's chosen people in sin and slavery, and hope for deliverance, clearly depicts a cycle of God's plan for man.

The teachings of salvation and new birth (often only thought of as being in the New Testament when Jesus hit the scene) began in the Old Testament – right from Genesis. The salvation process, from creation, fall, and redemption, can be described in the modern way as generation, degeneration, and regeneration, which is an intricate part of life. It is seen in all of nature's processes, either in plants, animals, or even in aspects of man's life. There is so much beauty and knowledge to take in from the book of Genesis, so hold on tight as you gain an understanding of God's divine design from the very beginning.

The History of Creation

The history of creation stretches one's mind as far as understanding God's thought processes, and it also leaves an undeniable warmth that stems from his love revealed in every verse. It helps you catch a glimpse at the answer to life's biggest question, "What's my purpose?". It paints the picture of creation in a completely new light, different from how other ancient texts or history fables described it. It shows creation for what it truly is: the existence of something from nothing.

God didn't just make; He *created*, and this can be deduced from the use of the Hebrew word "Bara" in the original text, which means to create, not just make or reform. Creation means bringing something to life that never existed in any other form. This act is unique to the person of God only. It is not born out of inferiority, accident, or chance but an intentional process that reveals and expresses God's nature.

To Life from Nothing – Genesis 1:1-31

In Genesis, you get to see the exceptional working of God's infinite power. In his creation of the world, He spoke, bringing into existence life and matter solely by the words of His mouth. The significance of this spoken word will be seen later in this chapter, but for now, delve into the *whys* of God's order of creation, the potential wisdom that can be gleaned from it, and its relevance in today's life.

• Genesis 1:1

It all began with the creation of the heavens and the Earth. The very first verse introduces the creative process involved in the birth of the world. The first three words, "In the beginning," show something profound. Although the actual date or time of the beginning is not known or recorded in the Bible, the focus is centered on the creation and the creator, emphasizing that God was there in the time of creation and was responsible for the creation. This gives more light to Jer. 10:16, which acknowledges God as the maker of all things. An understanding of this first verse is crucial as it sets the stage for the rest of all biblical events. After stating God as the pioneer of life and everything that exists, you are then introduced to the first recorded creation, heaven and Earth.

• Genesis 1, Verse 2

The next verse talks about the state of the world after God created it. There are many existing theories about Genesis 1, verse 2. Speculations have been made by some theologians that there was a world with form and structure before verse 2. They propose that something might have happened, possibly chaotic, that left the world in the formless and empty state as it was described in Genesis 2.

The arguments for their theory and against all others are based on a passage in the Bible in Isaiah 45:18, where the creation of the world is seen as a place formed and established to be inhabited and a place formed not in vain. Their arguments remain that if God had created the world in verse 1, He couldn't have created a world without form and void, and the scripture in Isaiah 45 serves as confirmation that, indeed, the world God created was one formed to be inhabited.

A deeper look also revealed that the Hebrew word used for the word "Void" in Genesis 1 is the same as the word used for the phrase "in vain" in Isaiah 45. It is then clearly seen in Isaiah 45, where God states that His creation was not made in vain.

A common concept that has spread since the inception of this idea is the "Gap theory." This theory strengthens the idea that there was a non-recorded chronological gap between the first verse of Genesis and the second. The discovery of old fossils, including fossils in extinction, is used to emphasize this theory, stating that these fossils belong to an existing time not recorded and the fact that something must have happened to the world to leave it in a structureless state. However, this theory can also be refuted when a keen look is taken at Rom 5:12, which clearly states that death came by Adam, meaning before Adam, there was no death. The presence of fossils means something died. This now leaves a question of how death can be before the existence of Adam, leaving this theory with holes that can not be explained. Regardless of the merit on which it is founded, the gap theory has unsuccessfully linked the existence of fossils to itself.

This inconsistency in facts now puts a dent in this theory. If death was absent before the fall of man and Adam came in verse 6, what became of the supposed world in between verses 1 and 2? Regardless of the merit the gap theory is founded upon, which is Isaiah 45:18, the theorists have been unable to use the discovery of fossils as further proof.

As you read on, you see the Bible describing the face of the deep as one covered with darkness. When you think of the word darkness, it can be seen as a form of resistance. Resistance to the move of the Holy Spirit, as you will see in the next line. The Spirit of God was present but would not move until the darkness was removed. Every time there needs to be some form of creation or re-creation, the Holy Spirit institutes it; He begins every work of birthing something new. The transforming of the world into something habitable and beautiful began when the Bible tells you, "... the Spirit of the Lord hovers over the face of the waters" – Genesis 1:2. The state of the world, in a simple word, was "Chaos," and the Holy Spirit needed to move upon it to move it from that fallen state to a state in which it is loved and appreciated.

- **Genesis 1, Verses 3-5**

Unlike later translations, the Hebrew version does a fantastic job of stating just how wonderful this creation was. It says, "Light be. Light was." There is no delay; the creation of light was instantaneous. For there to be order, light had to come. The importance of the coming of light first is seen further in 2 Cor 4:3-6. God called it forth by speaking. This shows that light outside of its physical concept has a spiritual dimension; it's not as you have come to know it. There was light and darkness long before the sun and moon were created, which are used today as the primary sources of light. When the new Earth and Heaven come, God alone will be the light, as there won't be any distinction in time, meaning no need for the sun or the moon. This is addressed in Rev 22:5.

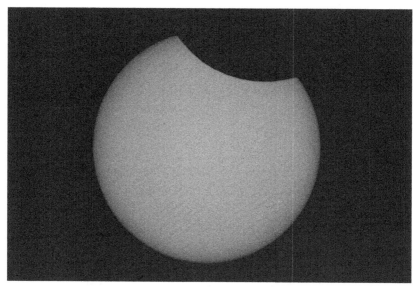

There will be no need for the sun or the moon in the new Earth and Heaven.
https://www.pexels.com/photo/sun-eclipse-9647389/

- ● **Genesis 1, Verses 6-8**

Discussions have risen on whether the creation of the world was orchestrated in six literal days or if there is a deeper meaning indicating a time system different from the one acknowledged today. With no fixed conclusion on this or concrete show of proof, it's safe to go along with the six days as your regular time system.

With the presence of light, God goes on to create an atmospheric division. He says, "Let there be a firmament in the midst of the waters, and let it divide the waters from the waters."– Genesis 1:6. Thus, God made the firmament and divided the waters which were under the firmament from the waters which were above the firmament, and it was so." A firmament is seen as a space or an expanse, and with its creation, we see the waters above separated from the waters below. This shows that the water present on land was separated from those in the form of vapor in the sky.

- ● **Genesis 1, Verses 9-13**

The third day shows the creation of all vegetation as the dry land is divided from the waters. This shows that the whole Earth was covered with water at first, and the separation gave room for life to grow. It is also interesting to know that life started or existed before the supposed "sustenance of life" was formed. This means that this vegetation didn't have the sun for their sustenance but rather must have nourished themselves on the light of God created in verse 3. This verse has also raised a lot of discussions as people question the possibility of vegetative life thriving in the absence of celestial bodies. In contrast, others use this possibility to refute the claim that the world was created in eons (a very long time or an indefinite period) rather than days.

- ● **Genesis 1, Verses 14-19**

All creations of God are beautiful, and some might even say magical. In all of creation, the most talked about and researched about would be the creations of the fourth day. On the fourth day, God said, "Let there be lights in the firmament of the heavens to divide the day from the night; and let them be for signs and seasons, and for days and years, and let them be for lights in the firmament of the heavens to give light on the earth;" and it was so -Gen 1:14-15. Then God made two great lights: the greater light to rule the day and the lesser light to rule the night. He made the stars also. God set them in the firmament of the Heavens to give light on the Earth, and to rule over the day and the night, and to divide the light from the darkness, and God saw that it was good. So, the evening and the morning were the fourth day.

In contemporary times, the symbolism of the sun, moon, and stars holds diverse meanings for different people. Still, in all of these, one sure thing is that, as a Christian, these heavenly bodies were placed in the firmament to serve you for signs and seasons. For as long as possible, mankind has been known to make use of the sun, moon, and stars as a source of direction and for measurement of time.

In certain cultures, you will see the sun serving as a symbol of vitality, enlightenment, and even hope. In others, you will see the moon embody things like mystery, the cycles of life, and sometimes tranquility, but never really peace because when you look at John 14:27, it talks about God being the giver of true peace. Multiple symbolisms of the stars also exist today to represent guidance.

The Celestial bodies are still a wide topic today, as they not only influence people's belief systems, daily reflections, or artistic expressions but do so on a much grander scale. It has been said that the US government invested 100 million dollars in the study of extraterrestrial intelligence. Beyond all of this significance to the world, it shows you the excellence of God's power. If the sun had stood some miles closer to Earth than it does, it would have been catastrophic. The same could be said if it stood farther from the Earth. Still, God, in his infinite wisdom, knew the perfect spot, and at the end of this creation, we can see the creator himself, God, acknowledge that it was good. This helps reduce the argument of spontaneous Earth, as nothing left to chance is ever perfect.

- **Genesis 1, Verses 20-23**

The creation of the birds of the air and creatures of the sea shows the crafting of a God who is detailed, precise, and purposeful. By taking a deep look at the diverse species of creatures in the air and, most especially, the sea, some of which are yet to be discovered, you'll get to see the depth of complexity mirrored in His craftsmanship. This should also reveal to you God's interest in the little details of your life. His work is always thoroughly and meticulously done; take a look at the various breeds in existence within a single species. A Beagle will never look like a golden retriever, nor will a Siberian husky look like a bulldog, although they are all dogs.

The creation of the birds of the air and creatures of the sea shows the crafting of a God who is detailed, precise, and purposeful.
https://www.pexels.com/photo/monochrome-photo-of-flock-of-flying-birds-1386454/

- **Genesis 1: Verses 24-25**

A look at the fifth creation and then the first part of the sixth creation should leave anyone who comes across it in awe and amazement. You may wonder why; well, take a look at the giraffe and the platypus. God sure knows how to have fun with diversity. The platypus is an egg-laying, otter-footed, beaver-tailed, duck-billed aquatic creature that's commonly found in the waters of Australia. The male of the species is also known to be venomous, and they are one of the few mammals with venom. This is an animal with the features of a bird, a reptile, and a regular mammal.

There are several other animals like the platypus, but a core moral of the story, as seen on the fifth day of creation, is the commandment for them to come forth according to their kind. The constant reiteration of this commandment over time shows the importance of uniqueness to God. Although you will see different variations within one species, it stops or ends within the species. A dog evolving into a lion is yet to happen– it probably never will!

In today's world, there have been few success stories of cross-breeding between different species, and all of that has only strengthened the proof of God's commandments. This is seen in cases of a horse and a donkey with a hybrid called a "mule" or that of a lion and a tiger, which has given rise to hybrids called "liger" and "tigon." The making of these hybrids did not come without limitations – and there's one crucial limitation: A major characteristic of living things is the ability to reproduce and procreate, but this important function of any living thing is lacking in these hybrids as they are either infertile or incapable of mating with a fellow hybrid, showing an end to any continuation of such species.

This understanding tells you to be you at all times and only aspire to embody God's unique characteristics for you and not something else.

- **Genesis 1, Verse 26**

Although the creation of man took place on the sixth day as well, you must take a look at this separately, as the creation of mankind and the instructions given to him apply to you directly. The opening statement by God, to create man in His image, is worth focusing on, as it simplifies the question on the lips of most people, but definitely in the heart of everyone, which is "What's my purpose?" or "Why am I here?". A solid understanding ofverse26 will provide that answer. Verse 26 says you are created in God's image, and, at each point, He addressed himself in the plural form, explaining the concept of the Trinity, which is God the Father, God the Son, and God the Holy Spirit. This we know because they were present at the time of creation.

To understand who you truly are and why you are here, you must first know who created you. A knowledge of God is a knowledge of yourself.

Life finds meaning and purpose when you know who created you and for what reason you were created. It's like staring into a clear stream or looking into a mirror; you are His replica, so when you see yourself, you see Him. Mankind alone has a different order from any other created being as only they possess a personality, spirituality, and conscience, which is their morality. Beyond this, they were also given the sole instruction and power to dominate. This is no coincidence; It is a consequence of being formed in His image. For this reason, His likeness is given to you as well.

The lessons in the story of creation are yet to be exhausted as fresh insights are being garnered daily. A continuous look into that chapter of the Bible will open you to new revelations that will influence your view on life and your everyday experiences.

The Garden of Eden: Adam and Eve

The Garden of Eden holds a lot of significance as it sets the stage for the events that played out later. Think of some of the most beautiful places in the world today: Machu Picchu, the Caribbean islands, Gobekli Tepe, etc. As beautiful as they are, they are nothing compared to the grandeur of the Garden of Eden. The Garden of Eden is much more than an oasis; it is a symbolic representation of the perfect harmony and beauty that should exist between God and mankind. It is a physical representation of our relationship with God, one of peace, love, joy, and unending happiness.

Adam and Eve in the garden of Eden.
https://www.flickr.com/photos/44534236@N00/16895519109

Moment of Reflection

1. What does the story of creation mean to you?
2. What are your thoughts on God's order of creation?
3. What aspects of God's creative process resonate with your personal beliefs or values?
4. How does knowing that you were created in the image of a supreme God influence your mind?
5. How do you view nature and other forms of life all around you in light of the story of creation?
6. After studying the lives of Adam and Eve, would you say you are like them in some ways?
7. When you think of what the Garden of Eden symbolizes, how do you relate it with what you understand perfection or paradise to be?
8. On topics like choices, temptation, and consequences, what lessons and insights did the story of Adam and Eve reveal on that?
9. Do you think you would have eaten the fruit if you were Eve? If yes, why? If No, why?

According to the Bible, the first-ever humans, Adam and Eve, were made on the sixth day of creation and placed in the garden to tend to it. From the creation story, upon mankind was the ability to dominate and subdue the Earth. At first, this was an instruction they continued without understanding. However, at the point of their temptation, they caved due to a lack of understanding, which reveals that deception is possible only in the face of ignorance. Although there are many other factors at play, the coming of the serpent to tempt Eve brought about the fall of man.

Chapter 2: Exodus and Liberation: Journeying with the Israelites

Walking through the genealogy of the Israelites and how they came to be in Egypt, you will find stories of Adam and Eve, Cain and Abel, Noah, Abraham and Sarah, Isaac and Jacob, and Joseph. The lives of these notable figures in Genesis shaped the frame for the next part of this adventure. The study of these lives reveals God's intentionality in bringing His promised people to a land He has prepared. Taking time to study the lives of each person mentioned above will also help in your understanding of the Bible as you progress, and you'll get to see God's method of dealing with His people.

The book of Exodus.
https://www.pexels.com/photo/close-up-shot-of-Bible-verse-5025563/

The story of the children of Israel in captivity under the rule of the Egyptians, their liberation, and their journey to the proposed promised land is one of great significance. A breakdown of the different timelines in the Bible would be incomplete without a detailed narration of the Israelites' journey. From the fulfillment of the prophecy, the exceeded time, the cry for help, the raising of a savior to deliver them, the processes of leaving, and the journey itself relates to the life of every individual, even in this present age. Here, you will learn lessons that will revolutionize your thought processes.

The Settlement

After the death of Joseph in Egypt, it seemed to the Israelites that their best days were behind them. However, from the previous chapter, one can easily deduce that God is completely intentional in His dealings and has a plan and set time for everything. The suffering and slavery of the Israelites in Egypt have been spoken of long before it happened.

In the time of Abraham, while he was yet called *Abram* in Genesis 15, God revealed to him that his descendants would be enslaved in a foreign land for four hundred (400) years. Although the prophecy stated 400 years, they remained in captivity for 430 years. There are many theories on why Genesis 15 says 400 years and 430 years were recorded in Exodus. One of these theories pins it on Moses' self-will to act before the set time when he killed an Egyptian. As of the time Moses killed the Egyptians, it was the 390th year, and they had ten more years until their liberation. Still, that act, which Moses might have seen as a way to help God or speed things up, was said to bring about the 30-year delay.

His actions towards the Egyptians led him to flee Egypt for the desert, where he stayed for 40 years until God visited him again. In today's modern age, the same is seen with most people; after getting a sense of God's will, they get so hasty to see it accomplished and fulfilled that they don't wait to find out God's method and pattern of accomplishing it, then messing it up in the process, or delaying it longer than anticipated. Learning to trust God wholeheartedly to see His will fulfilled in your life is key to growing your relationship with Him. When you take a look at Phil 1:6, you are reminded and assured that what He started, He most certainly can complete and not just complete, but also perfect in your life.

The Beginning of Liberation

The time God met Moses in the desert while he was tending to his father-in-law's sheep can be tagged as the start of the Israelites' freedom. Moses witnessed a bush that was ablaze but wasn't consumed. This incident shaped the rest of his life, as he later went on to deliver the children of Israel.

Moses being called by God before the burning bush.
https://www.flickr.com/photos/paullew/9304183235

In the presence of God before the burning bush, something significant happened that many people overlook. God didn't begin to speak to Moses as soon the bush started to burn; He waited until He saw that Moses indicated an interest in the sight before him. Moses said, "I'll now turn aside and see this great sight, why the bush does not burn."- Exo. 3:3. Moses was definitely not a stranger to fire as he must have understood the concept of fire on a consumable material like the bush, but his first reaction was not fear or doubt; it was interest. This singular act signaled God to speak. It is not certain if Moses' words were said out loud or in his heart; the important thing was that God acknowledged it, and afterward, he received his assignment and the direction on how to carry it out.

Other noteworthy moments at the burning bush scene are:

1. **The Call of Moses' Name:** He called his name twice. God wanted to establish that he knew him, just as He knows you and everything that concerns you.

2. **The Holy Ground:** God instructed Moses not to draw near until he had taken off his shoes. This shows that God is Holy and will not associate himself with any form of filth. This means you are to approach Him in this manner, not necessarily taking off your shoes but with a consciousness that you are coming before a Holy God. It also shows how you should see yourself. Seeing that you were created in His image, you must not associate with anything that is regarded as filth by your heavenly father.

3. **God's Introduction:** This is crucial every time God speaks. He does not leave it up to chance for the recipient to deduce or decide who He is. He states that it may be known. Here, He introduces himself as the God of his fathers, which also shows a relationship and covenant that goes back long before Moses.

The Message: Moses didn't leave for Egypt empty; he left with a word. God told him to tell them, "I AM". A knowledge of your affiliations and associations always has a way of influencing your approach toward a new task. Knowing you don't have to do something alone always comes with a level of confidence. It gets better when you are working with someone reliable, trustworthy, powerful, and influential. He also went with a message for the Children of Israel in Exodus 3:15-17:

> *"Moreover, God said to Moses, 'Thus you shall say to the children of Israel: 'The LORD God of your fathers, the God of Abraham, the God of Isaac, and the God of Jacob, has sent me to you. This is My name forever, and this is My memorial to all generations.' Go and gather the elders of Israel together, and say to them, 'The LORD God of your fathers, the God of Abraham, of Isaac, and of Jacob, appeared to me, saying, 'I have surely visited you and seen what is done to you in Egypt; and I have said I will bring you up out of the affliction of Egypt to the land of the Canaanites and the Hittites and the Amorites and the Perizzites and the Hivites and the Jebusites, to a land flowing with milk and honey.'"*

The Ten Plagues

Upon arrival in Egypt, Aaron spoke to the Elders of Israel on behalf of Moses. Then Moses performed the signs God had instructed him to do, and this made the people believe. With God, you are told to believe by faith and not by sight, but humans are reliant on their senses. They often must see, feel, and smell before they can believe, and God knew this, which is why He enabled Moses to perform the signs. This shows that results often go further than just words, so you must strive to have results in all you do.

With the children of Israel in order, Moses and Aaron proceeded to the palace to speak to Pharaoh. Moses was already pre-informed by God that even with the signs he would show, He would harden Pharaoh's heart not to release the Israelites, and it happened just as God had said. He hardened the heart of Pharaoh so He could send the ten plagues to show both the Israelites and Egyptians that He was the only true God.

With the hardening of Pharaoh's heart came a backlash against the Israelites as their labor intensified and became more strenuous. This bred doubt in the hearts of the children of Israel as they questioned whether the God of their fathers truly sent Moses. It is common for people to embrace doubts and questions and then second-guess every belief once things seem not to go the way they pictured.

The First Plague: Water Becomes Blood

Despite the weak attempts of Pharaoh and his magicians to refute and rebut the signs of God, God's excellence and majesty shone through. Rather than having a change of heart, Pharaoh hardened further, just as God had said he would. This goes to show that only the Holy Spirit can fully bring someone to a place of spiritual illumination and clarity. The plagues were a show by God to bring to naught and ridicule the supposed prominence of the Egyptian deities. The first plague was to make a mockery of the Egyptian god, Hapi. This was the god of the Egyptian river Nile, who was worshiped for his supposed gift of natural fertility to his followers. From verse 14, God, working through Aaron, turned the Nile River into blood, so the Egyptians had to dig the earth to source fresh water. God wasn't done, so He made it possible for Pharaoh's magicians to be able to replicate that act to some degree, and his heart was further hardened.

God turned the Nile River into blood to mock the Ancient Egyptians' god of the Nile, Hapi.

The Second Plague: Multiplication of Frogs

This next plague was a judgment against the Egyptian goddess of birth, Heqet, who was frog-headed. In ancient Egypt, frogs were revered and considered sacred. They represented symbols of generation and fertility. This god and her supposed powers were made a public joke as God caused the Nile to bring forth frogs that invaded every nook and cranny of Egypt aside from the dwelling place of the Israelites. They entered the Egyptian homes and took up all of their space, and when the frogs died, their bodies filled with stink were heaped up in huge piles all over the nation. It is exciting to read it the way the Bible puts it. The author of Exodus did not mince his words. No one was to be left out in Egypt, from their top-ranking officials to the lowest servants; frogs invaded everyone's personal space until they were losing their minds!

The Third Plague: Gnats

God took it up a notch in the third plague as the magicians of Egypt couldn't replicate it and openly declared before Pharaoh, "This is the finger of God. – Exo. 8:9" The third plague was a judgment against the deity Seth, who is the Egyptian god of the desert. God released gnats into all the land, displaying His sovereignty over sorcery and magic. The original Hebrew text did not say if these insects were gnats, but the Bible interpreted it to mean either gnats, lice, or some other type of insect, as the word used in the original text meant small insect. The acknowledgment of the magicians showed that they knew this was not just a natural phenomenal occurrence but rather the workings of a higher power. Regardless, Pharaoh's heart was still hardened.

The Fourth Plague: Swarm of Flies

Next came the flies, and there was a clear distinction between the land where the Israelites dwelled, Goshen, and the lands inhabited by the Egyptians. The Bible describes the plague as a grievous swarm of flies, and they terrorized the Egyptians without fail to the point at which Pharaoh sought out the help of Moses with a promise to let the children of Israel go. However, as you get to read the coming chapters in the Bible, you'll realize that Pharaoh didn't keep his promise. This plague was a judgment brought on Uatchit, the god of flies. God rains down judgment on the so-called gods of the Egyptians to show Pharaoh and his people that there is only one true living God.

The Fifth Plague: Death of Livestock

After the fourth plague ended, Pharoah went back on his promise to let the children of Israel go. The fifth plague was brought against two Egyptian gods, who were both depicted as cattle, the god Apis and the goddess Hathor. God, through Moses and Aaron, caused the death of all livestock belonging to the Egyptians, bringing no harm to those of the children of Israel. This shows God's steady hand of protection over those who choose to obey him. This is not just protection but an all-around provision for His Children. Matt. 5:45 talks about God causing rain to fall and the sun to shine on both the just and unjust, but it gets better for those who choose to acknowledge Him as Father and Lord.

The Sixth Plague: Boils

The boils of the sixth plague were intense. It is recorded in the scriptures that the magicians of Egypt could not stand before Pharaoh because they were also inflicted with the same affliction as all the other Egyptians. This significantly showed that the help the Egyptians had, or thought they had, from the magicians failed. This is applicable to daily living as well. However, it's not wrong to rely on others; there's a limit to the help they can offer, but when working with God, there are no fears of being left alone because He always comes through.

The Egyptian gods Sunu, Sekhmet, and Isis were the focus of the sixth judgment. These gods represented health, wellness, and disease, so boils were brought to make a mockery of their supposed power.

The Seventh Plague: Hail

God sent a message to Pharaoh beforehand to prepare him for this plague, and still, his heart remained hardened, just as God had said. God made it known that He was God, and there was none like him on all the earth. God also informed Pharoah that His presence on the throne was because of him, but he took it for granted. The hail brought judgment on Osiris, Set, and Nut, the gods of crop fertility, storm, and sky, respectively. So disastrous was the hail that it came with fire, destroying everything left in its wake. God went as far as warning Pharaoh to bring in and store everything alive as the hail would wipe them all out. At this point, division arose among the Egyptians. Some, in fear, went ahead and heeded the words of God through Moses by bringing in their servants, crops, and livestock in the field, while others refused, and hail came and consumed everything left outdoors.

The Eighth Plague: Locust

Locusts were brought upon the Egyptians, and all the late-season crops, like wheat and spelt, which were left behind after the barley was taken, were eaten up by the locust. Their gods, Osiris and Nut, were ridiculed and judged here, showing God's power. Just as He told Moses, His children would be able to tell their children of His power they witnessed and the diverse signs they saw.

The Plague of Locusts.

The Ninth Plague: Darkness

The intensity of the darkness of the ninth plague was so much that the darkness was described as something that could be felt. It was judgment brought upon the god of light or the sun god, Re or Amon-Ra. Pharaoh himself was the symbol of this god. To the Egyptians, the sun's rising and setting signified life and death, meaning that whenever the sun rose in the morning, it meant life to the ancient Egyptians. When it set, it meant death. Similar to the third and sixth plagues, this plague came without any warning, isolating the Egyptians not only from the Israelites but also from themselves. The scripture says that no one could move from the point they were because of the severity of this plague.

By God taking over and subjecting unearthly darkness on their land, He was declaring ultimate supremacy over every other god, bringing the Egyptian top god into judgment and confining him to the realm of death. It only makes sense with this understanding that the plague of death would come next.

The Tenth Plague: Death of the Firstborn

The death of the firstborns meant and represented a lot. Firstly, firstborns are known to represent new beginnings, pride, hope, and joy; the death of the firstborns shows that this was taken away from the Egyptians. As the Bible describes it, "... great wailing would be heard from them" (Exodus 11:6) at the time that plague would come. Here comes the contrast: in the city of Goshen, the dwelling place of the Israelites, there was total serenity and tranquility; as God said, not even a dog would bark.

A deeper meaning also lies in the dog illustration used, as this final plague also brought judgment on the Egyptian god of the dead or the embalming god, Anubis, depicted as a dog. This reveals God's deliverance and salvation that brings a peace no one can understand – as seen later in the New Testament in Philippians 4:7. The death of the firstborns pushed Pharaoh to let the children of Israel go, just as God had said. The Israelites adhered to all the instructions God gave them on their exit from Egypt and caused them to be favorably disposed towards the Egyptians, and they plundered the land, leaving with great spoils.

This final plague also brought judgment on the Egyptian god of the dead, Anubis.
See page for author, CC0, via Wikimedia Commons.
*https://commons.wikimedia.org/wiki/File:The_Sacred_Books_and_Early_Literature_of_the_Eas
t,_vol._2,_pg._208-209,_Anubis.jpg*

Road to Freedom

There was immense joy and excitement for the Israelites as they began their journey through the wilderness, but this joy was short-lived, as, after a while of journeying, the Egyptians went after them. Pharaoh's heart and that of his servants hardened towards the children of Israel, and they regretted letting them go and pursued after them in hopes of getting them back. However, God showed up again for His people; He drowned the Egyptians when He parted the Red Sea through the rod of His servant Moses. This singular act holds so much significance today for believers as it indicates complete salvation and total deliverance from any oppressor. God didn't leave anything up to time and chance but rather settled the matter once and for all, declaring total freedom for His people.

Moment of Reflection

1. Which of the ten plagues impressed you the most, and why?

2. The Children of Israel reacted to the increase in labor after Moses first met with Pharoah. What is usually your first disposition towards God when you face challenges? How do you gauge your faith in God based on your answer?

3. Based on God's dealings with the Israelites and the Egyptians, how do you see the nature of God?

4. Write down two characteristics of God that He displayed in the book of Exodus, and think about how these characteristics can affect your life.

God is very precise and intentional about everything He does. This is seen in how He meticulously arranged and ordered the ten plagues. When God works, He works on all fronts, never leaving any stone unturned. Any victory in God is always total victory!

Chapter 3: The Wisdom of Psalms and Proverbs: Guidance for Everyday Living

The "Fear of the Lord" is the core concept of the Bible, and all the teachings and exhortations you will find are centered around it. This concept is very much emphasized in the book of Psalms and Proverbs, with the theme focused on "Wisdom" and "Worship" more than any other book. Life as a Christian is meant to be lived in total worship of God through His wisdom, which makes these books so fascinating. A study of the book of Psalms will leave you in complete awe and reverence of God. It puts your heart in a posture of gratitude and worship primarily for God's role as your Creator, Father, Helper, and so much more. At the same time, the book of Proverbs teaches you how to live a life that pleases God. It addresses key areas of your life and will equip you with the wisdom to go about them. Aside from the book of Genesis, another good place to begin the study of the Bible would be the books of Psalms and Proverbs.

The book of Psalms.

These are the only two books known to have multiple authors. The rich experiences of the different authors make for an amazing overlay of the chapters in these books. However, of all these authors, two stand out: King David of the Book of Psalms and King Solomon, King David's son of the Book of Proverbs.

When in doubt, joy, fear, excitement, pain, love, anguish, despair, faith, etc., these books will help to guide your heart. There is always a passage to address your current needs, give you insight, and uplift your spirit. They address all your emotions and provide you with instructions for righteous living. Below are many insights and key themes of this book.

Psalms: A Harmony of Hearts and Hymns

The book of Psalms is the expression of a man's heart. At any point in his life, it shows his connection to one source: God. This book is a compilation of songs; each lyrical poem is a revelation of the human heart in worship of God. Some of the authors of these songs in Psalms are mentioned at the start of the song in that chapter, while the authors of others are not. Some of the authors include King David, who wrote the most by authoring seventy-three (73) chapters, Moses, Aspha, the descendants of Korah, King Solomon, Herman the Ezrahite, and Ethan.

The book fully represents the meaning of its name, Psalms, which means "Praise" or "Songs of Praise," or its original name, which is the Hebrew word "Tehillim," meaning "Praise songs." It is composed of reflections, meditations, instructions, prayers for help, thanksgiving songs, hymns, corporate prayers for help, etc. Regardless of the other different genres seen in Psalms, its central focus is the praise and worship of God.

The book of Psalms spans nearly a thousand years, from the time of Moses to the post-exilic season in Babylon. Aside from being the longest book in the Bible and covering a diverse range of topics from creation, God's salvation, judgment, the kingdom of God, Israel's history, the law of life, the mystery of human conditions, and so much more, it is also the most read book of the Old Testament. It contains a total of 150 lyrical compositions that explore man's relationship with God, whether a celebration of victory, a cry for help, a search for comfort in trials, or a pouring out of one's soul in prayers.

In Matthew 22: 37, Jesus' teaching tells everyone that the greatest commandment is to love the Lord your God with all your heart, all your soul, and all your mind. A Christian in true pursuit of carrying out this commandment will turn to the book of Psalms, as it shows how to love God with total courage, consciousness, and intellect.

Proverbs: Wisdom Snapshots

In slight contrast, the book of Proverbs, attributed largely to King Solomon, beyond its wise sayings, provides insight into how to live. Although there are other authors involved in the compilation of this book, King Solomon serves as the principal author, having written a significant portion. He is renowned for his wisdom and wrote over 3,000 proverbs and over 1,005 songs. He was the third King of Israel after the era of judges when the Israelites had settled in Cannan. He ascended the throne at an early age after his Father, King David, died. Still, in his young and inexperienced state, he did something extremely wise for which he was rewarded greatly by God.

In a bid to seek help on how to lead God's people, Solomon offered a huge sacrifice to God, which led to God asking him to name whatever he wanted. Solomon asked for wisdom on how best to rule and lead God's people. This singular request pleased God, and He gave him his heart's desire and included everything else: wealth, fame, and peace from his enemies. This action gave Israel its longest reign of peace, which was 40 years without conflict or strife with other nations.

Solomon poured out this wisdom in the book of Proverbs. This book is characterized by practical advice on how to live a righteous and fulfilling life. It is so great that its teachings are not limited to those of a certain demographic, race, ethnicity, nativity, or class. Its teachings are so instrumental to life that they resonate with all who seek it out.

Proverbs covers a wide array of subjects vital for everyday living, like the importance and power of words, the value of pursuing knowledge and understanding, why it's important to conduct oneself ethically, how to make sound decisions, how to foster good relationships, stop a bad habit, learn a good habit, have an understanding of the principles that define a life laid out in total reverence to God, etc. You can always find something helpful in proverbs, and its insights are presented in nuggets, short and memorable, for easy assimilation and remembrance.

Inasmuch as this book shows the wisdom of life during the time of King Solomon, its value has not at all depreciated; it is still very much applicable in your everyday life today. The primary purpose of the book of Proverbs is to show you the path to wisdom, which is through the fear of the Lord. This is confirmed in the constant usage of the phrase "the fear of God" within the pages, more than any other book in the Bible.

An amazing feature you will notice as you study the book of Proverbs is its beauty in communicating this wisdom to its readers through the use of discourse and personification. It reveals a balance between man's choices and God's laws, showing how the sovereignty of God can harmonize with the free will of man. A conclusion you are bound to draw from your study of this book is that true wisdom can only be attained when a man is right with God, and that is the central focus of Proverbs. From Proverbs' perspective, a knowledgeable, smart, and intelligent man without God is devoid of wisdom.

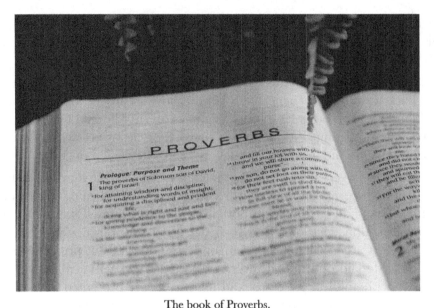

The book of Proverbs.
https://www.pexels.com/photo/close-up-shot-of-book-of-proverbs-11877603/

Psalms and Proverbs: The Interlink

These two books, although distinct, offer complementary views or perspectives on key subjects of life, faith, and wisdom. Psalms consist primarily of poetic expressions of praise, lament, and worship, while Proverbs is more in line with practical wisdom. These different writing styles communicate similar messages. You will get to see how the insights highlighted repeatedly in these books are vital for your everyday living and how they resonate with the challenges faced in today's modern world.

A look at the historical and cultural context of Psalms and Proverbs reveals their enduring appeal. The book of Psalms, penned centuries ago, opens you up to the evolving societal and religious shifts seen in ancient Israel. Chapter by chapter, you will see how it successfully captures the triumphs, tragedies, and spiritual yearnings of the nation of Israel. This serves as a testament to man's eternal pursuit of connection with the divine. In comparison, Proverbs, which is often attributed to the time of the reign of King Solomon, immerses you in the wisdom of the ancient near East traditions. Proverbs' aphorisms and emphasis on practical wisdom are short and to the point, which differs from the expressive style of psalms. Culturally, the influence of the teachings in Psalms and Proverbs transcends the boundaries of religion alone. It cuts across a myriad of other fields, such as literature, philosophy, art, music, etc., throughout diverse cultures. The universal and enduring nature of their themes has served as wellsprings of inspiration for countless philosophers, writers, literature experts, artists, etc., across the expanse of human history. The way emotions are explored in these two books, especially Psalms and the pragmatic dispensation of insights in Proverbs, resonates universally, serving as a bridge for the gaps that exist among people from varied backgrounds, proving relevant in the different cultural and religious landscapes.

Beyond the artistic and cultural impact of Psalms and Proverbs, they have become subjects of profound inquiry by many scholars. Theological luminaries, Biblical scholars, and literary critics have engaged in a comprehensive examination of these texts, coming at them from various perspectives to unveil their different dimensions, both historical, literary, and theological. This interdisciplinary approach will not only deepen your comprehension of Psalms and Proverbs but will also illuminate their contextual significance. The scholarly interpretations stretch far beyond the confines of academia, providing you with insights that render these ancient texts not only accessible but profoundly relevant to contemporary issues and concerns. As a result, Psalms and Proverbs continue to serve as beacons of wisdom, guiding modern audiences such as yourself through the intricate terrain of this life with timeless and universal applicability.

Thematic Look at Psalms and Proverbs

Much has been said about the immense impact of the books of Psalms and Proverbs in your life today. In this section, we look at some of the key themes which are a part of everyday life.

Wisdom in Adversity

Adversity in life is not a new concept. Just as there are days of prosperity, days of adversity are just around the corner. This is not a shot at pessimism; it's how the world works. It is expressed in the story of the seven years of abundance and want during the time of Joseph in Genesis 41. One of each is always bound to happen at any given point in a man's life. Your question should be, what does God's word have to say about His children in the days of adversity, and what wisdom can be gleaned from these books for such times?

You will experience adversity, but you should never be afraid.
https://unsplash.com/photos/man-kneeling-down-near-shore-bEbqpPeHEM4

The Bible makes it clear that as a Christian, you will experience adversity, but you shouldn't worry, be afraid, or cower; rather, you should be courageous because Christ Jesus, your Lord, has overcome the world. It is with this understanding that you draw your victory. This is seen in John 16, verse 33, and Proverbs instructs believers about adversity. In verse 10 of chapter 24 in Proverbs, you are encouraged to persevere always and be strong in the day of adversity, meaning it will come, but your approach to it will determine how you come out of it-victorious or defeated. This verse teaches you to be resilient and determined when you are confronted with different challenges.

Similarly, this understanding is stretched further in Psalms. For example, various passages like Psalm 34, verses 17-18, show the author expressing a deep emotional response to adversity but not losing heart. Rather than fret in the face of adversity, their cry is turned towards their helper, God. He hears them and provides comfort to them from their troubles. The beauty of Psalms is that it doesn't shy away from the pain experienced during tough times; neither does it dwell on it solely. Instead, it acknowledges the struggle while relying on a higher power, God, for strength and deliverance.

This approach to adversity is just as effective today. Instead of wallowing in fear and doubt, which breeds depression in the face of challenges, you should draw wisdom from Psalms and Proverbs by turning to God for strength to help you sail through victoriously with joy. It's just like the story of a man called Job in the Bible, whom Satan tormented with a great adversary to get him to turn away from God and lose faith. However, Job reacted in one of the most impressive ways possible: When he lost all he had, he said, "... the Lord gives, and the Lord takes. Blessed be the name of the Lord – Job 1:21". So, you see, it's possible to be joyful even amid distress. Notice the word joyful and not happy: Happiness is a result of the physically pleasurable things around you, while joy stems from an inner peace from God not influenced by your surroundings or circumstances.

Challenges indeed differ from person to person, but the primary method of victory is the same for everyone: turn to God, draw strength, approach the challenge in Faith with joy, and enjoy your victory. Psalm 34:19 and Proverbs 3:5-6 also shed further light on a Christian's idea of adversity, "The righteous person may have many troubles, but the LORD delivers him from them all" and "Trust in the LORD with all your heart and lean not on your understanding; in all your ways submit to him, and he will make your paths straight." Together, these books offer a comprehensive view of facing adversity with a combination of practical wisdom from Proverbs and the emotional and spiritual perspective found in Psalms. It is a holistic approach that encourages both mental fortitude and spiritual reliance during challenging times.

The Power of Words

Proverbs 18:21 says, "Life and death are in the power of the tongue." This verse encapsulates everything you would read in this whole section. It highlights the impact that the words you say can have on your life. There are no limits to how far your words can go or how deep into the nooks and crannies of your life they can reach. This verse also underscores the responsibilities that come with speaking and your ability to communicate, urging you to be careful in your usage of words.

A similar discussion on the power of words is also seen in Psalms in its usual poetic form. In Psalms 141:3, the Psalmist makes a plea to God, asking him to set a guard over his mouth and to keep watch over his lips. Although in a different style to Proverbs, it has a similar message. With the infusion of emotions, you can sense the desperation of his words as you read, which shows his understanding of the power of words.

Proverbs 16:24 says, "Gracious words are a honeycomb, sweet to the soul and healing to the bones." in Proverbs 15:4, "The soothing tongue is a tree of life, but a perverse tongue crushes the spirit." This imagery vividly contrasts the life-giving power of gentle, comforting words with the destructive force of harsh, hurtful speech. A read through Psalms and Proverbs highlights the profound influence of words in all aspects of your life. You are urged to wield your words with care, knowing the weight it carries. When you align your speech to bring life, you are pleasing God and working in the fear of Him.

Gracious words are compared to the sweetness of honeycomb in the book of Proverbs.
https://www.pexels.com/photo/delicious-honeycomb-filled-with-honey-8105066/

Pursuit of Righteousness

A pursuit of righteousness is synonymous with an honorable and flourishing life. Still, outside its numerous benefits, it is a call to all Christians. Proverbs 21:21 tells you that "Whoever pursues righteousness and love will find not only life but prosperity and honor." The book of Psalms not only addresses the topic of righteousness multiple times, but this discourse sets the tone for the book in general. The first three verses of the Psalm talk about the lifestyle of a man living in righteousness and not pursuing ungodliness.

Psalm 1:1-3 says,

> *"Blessed is the man that walketh not in the counsel of the ungodly, nor standeth in the way of sinners, nor sitteth in the seat of the scornful. But his delight is in the law of the Lord; and in his law doth he meditates day and night. And he shall be like a tree planted by the rivers of water, that bringeth forth his fruit in his season; his leaf also shall not wither; and whatsoever he doeth shall prosper."*

In this verse, the concept of righteousness is connected to a life deeply rooted in God's word; such a life always results in productivity, stability, and prosperity. Choosing to be honorable is always vital to the life of a believer walking with God. It might seem easier to alter the numbers at work, cheat on a test, tell a lie, or gossip about a friend, but these things do not align with your principles as a believer, so they shouldn't be found in or around you.

Furthermore, Proverbs 11:19 provides a contrast between the outcomes of righteousness and wickedness: "Truly the righteous attain life, but whoever pursues evil finds death." This close comparison points out the transformative impact of choosing the path of righteousness. In comparison with Psalms, Psalm 34:15 echoes this sentiment when it says, "The eyes of the Lord are on the righteous, and his ears are attentive to their cry." You receive this assurance that reflects God's divine connection with you as you earnestly pursue righteousness.

Expanding on the pursuit of righteousness, Proverbs 21:3 states, "To do what is right and just is more acceptable to the Lord than sacrifice." This verse emphasizes the intrinsic value of righteous actions over external rituals. It's not really about the nice things you say; the posture of your heart matters more to God, as you can see within this verse. This also relates to a chapter in Psalms that asks the question, "Who is fit to inquire of God and who is fit to live on his Holy Mountain"- Psalm 15:1. The answer then goes on to describe the characteristics of a righteous man as one who fits the bill in this context.

Righteousness is a path that leads to life. As you study the books of Psalms and Proverbs, you will discover more verses that touch on this topic, giving you a better understanding of righteousness. This pursuit is an active, intentional journey towards the right and just thing in the sight of God. Psalm 119:1-2 says, "Blessed are those whose ways are blameless, who walk according to the law of the LORD. Blessed are those who keep his statutes and seek him with all their heart."

Moments of Reflection

1. If you were asked to mention the one thing you desire the most now, just like Solomon, what would it be?

2. Psalms often explore a range of emotions, from joy to sorrow. Which Psalm do you find most relatable to your current feelings or life situation? Why?

3. Reflect on a mistake or lesson learned in your life. How does the concept of learning through mistakes, emphasized in Proverbs, resonate with your experiences?

4. Proverbs offer practical wisdom for daily living. What proverbial advice do you find particularly relevant to a current situation or decision you're facing? How might applying this wisdom impact your choices?

One thing is guaranteed: a study of the books of Psalms and Proverbs will leave you better than it found you. You have the assurance of a renewed way of thinking. You can begin to take actionable steps from the lessons of these books that reshape your choices and habits.

Chapter 4: The Life and Teachings of Jesus

Learning about the life of Jesus and His teachings is beyond the purpose of acquiring knowledge. It guides your understanding of God and reveals His heart about life's purpose, which in turn causes a total transformation in your heart. These stories and teachings are not time-bound, as their lessons are still very relatable in today's contemporary world. It doesn't matter if you're starting on your Bible journey; a view into Jesus' life and teachings will give you a new perspective of life, fill your heart with the boldness to face trials and challenges, and equip you with faith and expectation for His promised end to all His Children. As you go into the pages of this chapter, get ready to yearn for a deeper relationship with God.

The birth of Jesus.
https://www.pexels.com/photo/holy-family-figurines-6244101/

The Birth of Jesus

The birth of Jesus is so significant that every event, story, and teaching right from the start of Genesis, all through the books of the Old Testament into the New Testament, were preparations for the coming of the Messiah, Jesus. The prophecies of His birth and life have been recounted centuries before His arrival. You can consider the manifestation of His birth as a collision of the supernatural and natural, an event divinely orchestrated by God. It all began with Mary, a young virgin woman engaged to a man in the small town of Nazareth, who finds favor in the sight of God and receives a visit from an angel. The angel came with the news of her being chosen to bear the savior of the whole world, the son of God. Can you stop to imagine Mary's possible thoughts and reactions to such news?

However, another person who really mattered was her fiancé, Joseph, and God made it possible for him to stay by her side as this miracle unfolded. He was also visited by an angel and instructed by God not to put Mary away but to stay with her because the child was from the Holy Spirit.

In Luke chapter one, Mary, still in the process of coming to terms with this divine revelation, paid a visit to her relative, Elizabeth, who was heavily pregnant. This visitation had more significance than simply two relatives paying each other visits. During this visit, the baby in Elizabeth's womb, whom you will know to be John the Baptist, filled with the spirit of God right from the womb, instantly recognized the presence of His Lord, Jesus, in the womb of Mary and leaped for joy. Understanding the sign, Elizabeth recognizes the significance of Mary's role in the grand scheme of God's divine plan.

Around the time of the conception of Jesus in chapter 2 of Matthew, the Bible spoke about three wise men who can be regarded today as scholars or astronomers. These wise men coming from the east were said to receive a sign from a star and chose to follow that star, leading them to Judea. Coming from a long distance across vast landscapes, they sought the King whose star they saw appear one night, and it led them to Jesus.

The birth of Jesus in a manger is beyond the result of an earthly activity; it wasn't just the by-product of an overcrowded inn during a tax census. The simplicity of the stables was an indication of God's humility to take on the form of man and His willingness to become human to help men right their wrongs. The birth of Jesus wasn't merely a historical event; the lessons from Mary's courage, the wise men's journey, the political turbulence, and Joseph's faith all sum up the reality of the supernatural.

Meanwhile, on the political stage, Herod, the ruler of Judea, learned of the birth of a king through the wise men and felt a threat to his position as King. In Matthew 2, Herod issued a decree that all male children under the age of two born in Bethlehem were to be killed due to the threat posed by the birth of Jesus.

The Miracles of Jesus

After His birth, Joseph, being warned by an angel in a dream, fled with Mary and Jesus to Egypt until the death of King Herod. However, in fear that Herod's son might continue in the footsteps of his father, Joseph didn't return to Judea but moved to the land of Galilee, to the small city of Nazareth, where Jesus grew up until the start of His ministry at the age of 30. From His conception in a humble stable to His studies at the temple with the scholars when He was 12, and up until his baptism by John at the age of 30, the Bible recorded that Jesus grew in wisdom and favor. When the time came for Him to step into the forefront of public life, in the fulfillment of the will of God upon Him, He began to do remarkable things. Jesus performed diverse miracles, some of which will be discussed here and others you will come to know about as you go deeper into your study of God's word.

You must understand just how extraordinary His signs were in a time when the multiple factors at play were physical ailments, political turbulence, and economic challenges. The coming Messiah was their only beacon of hope. Just like Herod, they all thought that being the promised Messiah, Jesus was coming to free them from Roman rule and rule them as a king, but Jesus had far better plans. His presence was to offer them hope, far beyond their present struggles, and a life of freedom, then and after, to all who accepted Him.

All through the four gospels, you will find Jesus healing the sick, as many came to Him for healing. This act was not just a show of power but rather Jesus' sincere response to the cries of His people in desperate need of restoration, as they were in a parlous situation with the Romans. As Jesus walked among the people, turning water into wine, multiplying loaves and fishes, and even raising the dead, you will see a great significance in each of those acts. It wasn't just about the magnificence of the miracles but the recipients of these miracles. Every person in each miracle was just a regular individual going about their lives with their daily struggles, hoping for some sort of deliverance. Jesus came at the right time when they were desperately in need of a miracle.

Feeding of the Crowd

One of the extraordinary feats accomplished by Jesus was the feeding of the five and four thousand. This account of the multiplication of fish and bread was recorded in four books of the Bible: Mattew, Mark, Luke, and John. In this particular experience, Jesus, while teaching, was moved with compassion for the crowd, as they had been with Him for three days in the wilderness without anything to eat. Not wanting to send them home on an empty stomach, Jesus resolved to feed them.

However, His disciples informed Him that only five loaves of bread and two fishes were available. Jesus was not moved by the insignificant quantity of food in comparison to the number of persons present. He asked that the disciples make the people sit in a particular order, took the bread and fish, and gave thanks to God. After Jesus had finished, He gave it back to His disciples to distribute to the people, and there was more than enough to go around. The five loaves of bread and two fishes were successfully distributed among five thousand people who ate their fill, with twelve baskets of food left over.

Jesus feeding five thousand people.
https://www.flickr.com/photos/paullew/4811299.5663

This miracle revealed that Jesus wasn't only interested in the spiritual growth of His people, as He had done for the past three days. He was also interested in their physical needs as well. It also showed His divine power over scarcity as a symbol of God's supernatural abundance.

Turning Water to Wine

Another amazing miracle was at a wedding feast, where Jesus turned water into wine. Jesus was present at a wedding in Cana, and the wine being used for guests ran out while the wedding was still in full swing. This led those present to seek help from Mary, Jesus's mother, on what to do. Knowing who her son was, she brought it up to Him, although Jesus revealed it wasn't time for Him to perform such manifestations.

However, being moved with compassion, He instructed the servants to fill up six empty stone jars with water and serve them to the guests. They heeded Jesus' instruction, and the water in the jars became wine. The guest acknowledged that the wine was better than the first batch that was served when they asked, "Why have you saved the best for last?" (It was customary to serve the best wine first at any gathering, so when the guests were drunk with the good wine, they would not be able to tell the difference!)

Jesus turned water into wine.
https://www.pexels.com/photo/wine-glass-with-red-wine-391213/

This event is considered Jesus' first public miracle, which symbolizes His divine authority over even the elements of nature. The abundance and quality of the wine produced in this miracle also show Jesus' ability to bring about joy and richness even in the most unexpected situations.

The Woman with the Issue of Blood

This Bible revealed the struggle of a woman who had lived with a particular condition for twelve years and had spent all her money on non-profitable visits to physicians, yet it continued to worsen. While in the middle of her pain from the bleeding, she hears of Jesus and, in faith, goes to Him for her healing. The beautiful thing about this miracle was the absence of Jesus laying His hands on her; rather, she was healed by her faith, which was clearly displayed in her actions. She believed all she had to do to get her healing was to touch Jesus' cloak. Not minding the pressure from the crowds around Jesus, she pressed until she reached the hem of Jesus' garment. As she touched the garment, the bleeding dried up instantly, and it was recorded that Jesus immediately knew that virtue had gone out of Him. After Jesus had found her in the crowd, He was impressed by her level of faith and declared that her faith had made her well in Mark 5:34: "Daughter, your faith has made you well; go in peace and be healed of your disease."

This miracle illustrates Jesus' compassion towards the sick, His willingness to respond to faith, and His power to heal. It also emphasizes the importance of faith and persistence in seeking a miracle.

These miracles and many more contributed to the spread of His fame across the land – tales of a man who defied the laws of nature, who brought relief to the sick, and who challenged the societal order. These were not just a series of events; rather, they were events that unfolded in response to the needs and challenges of the time in ancient Judea.

Jesus' Ministry and Teachings

The diverse miracles are not the only things noted about the life of Jesus. His teachings formed a core part of Christianity today, and it would be incomplete to look at the life of Jesus without buttressing the lessons He taught. There were no limits on the subjects covered in Jesus's teachings. He covered every area of life: salvation, the kingdom of God, faith, prayers, humility, money, possessions, love and compassion, repentance, forgiveness, judgment, the end times, etc. Either directly or through the use of parables, Jesus always gave vital life lessons. He came to show men how to live a purposeful life effortlessly. The trees on the earth, the fishes in the sea, and the birds of the sky don't struggle to thrive in their natural habitat, and that was what Jesus came to do, showing us how to live a life of total worship to God seamlessly, and this He communicated through His teachings.

Here are some of Jesus' teachings in Parables and the insights to be gleaned from them;

The Parable of the Good Samaritan

In this parable, Jesus tells the story of a man who was attacked by robbers on his way from Jerusalem to Jericho and solicited help from passersby, and none but one would help him. Jesus made us know that the only person who volunteered to help was a Samaritan, while the others who wouldn't stop to help were a Levite and a Jewish priest. This statement alone has great tribal significance. In those times, the Jews and Samaritans were enemies. The Samaritan laid him on his horse, took him to an inn, and paid for his medical bills. The lessons are clear: compassion knows no boundaries, regardless of tribe, race, ethnicity, nationality, etc. Love should always come first. Today, this parable challenges you to extend kindness and care to all, regardless of societal divisions or differences.

The Parable of the Prodigal Son

Jesus shares the story of a wayward son welcomed home by a loving father. A man had two sons, and his second son requested his inheritance, which he obliged. His son goes away and squanders his part of the inheritance and is left with nothing to the point of being willing to eat with the pigs. In that state of soberness, repentance, and reflection, the son returned home to his father. He begged to be taken back, even as a servant. The father welcomed him and held a feast in his honor.

The parable emphasizes God's unconditional love and forgiveness as a father to His children. Today, it serves as a reminder that, no matter your past, you can always return to the open arms of a forgiving and compassionate God who is ever ready to receive you.

The Parable of the Mustard Seed

In this parable, Jesus uses the analogy of a mustard seed to explain the importance and significance of humble or small beginnings. The mustard seed, when sown, is considerably small. Still, when given time, it grows into a large plant that contributes greatly to its environment. Jesus teaches about the Kingdom of God, which started small but flourished remarkably. The significance today lies in the transformative power of small acts and humble beginnings. It serves as a reminder that even the smallest efforts can have a profound impact.

The Parable of the Lost Sheep

In this parable, Jesus spoke of a shepherd who had a hundred sheep and lost one. Out of love for the one, he leaves the ninety-nine to find the one lost sheep. Some might consider it foolish, but it shows great love, especially when you see yourself as the one. It conveys God's relentless pursuit of each individual. Today, it serves as an encouragement to love and value everyone. Remember, no one is beyond redemption or unworthy of God's love.

The Parable of the Sower

In this parable, a sower went about sowing on a particular day. As he sowed, Jesus explained that the seeds fell on different grounds, by the wayside, among thorns, on stony grounds, and on good and fertile soil. Due to the different foundations of the seeds, they all ended differently. Birds ate up the ones by the wayside. The seeds among thorns sprang up but were choked by the thorns. Seeds on stony ground grew up fast, but because of inadequate depth of soil for a good foundation, the sun scorched the plants. Finally, the ones that fell on good and fertile ground thrived and produced a harvest thirty-, sixty-, and a hundred-fold!

Jesus used this metaphor of different soils to explain how Christians receive the word of God at different times. This parable teaches the importance of cultivating a heart that is always receptive to God's word. This parable should serve as a challenge to always strive for a heart that will bear lasting fruits.

The Crucifixion and Resurrection

The crucifixion and resurrection of Jesus will forever shape the course of history. In a time when the Romans ruled the Jews, there were many complexities surrounding religion, societal demands, and expectations. The use of crucifixion as a form of punishment was reserved for the most heinous of criminals because of how brutal it was. Following the weight of Jesus' ministry, He was bound to make some enemies, especially among people who were not pleased with His methods and teachings. They conspired and had Him arrested on the basis of many false allegations. Jesus, being innocent, faced the agony of the cross. Despite being the son of God, the Bible revealed that He wasn't immune to the pain and shame of the cross. This was demonstrated when Jesus was recorded praying to God that He may not face the judgment of the cross in the book of Matt. 26:39; "Father, if it's possible, let this cup pass from me; nevertheless, not as I will, but as you will." However, His crucifixion wasn't merely a cruel event of injustice among men and a challenge to the societal norms and religious expectations of that era. It was also a convergence of His divine sacrifice. Beyond the spiritual significance, it shows the harsh realities of Roman oppression and the great lengths the spiritual leaders of old were willing to go to preserve their beliefs.

Jesus's crucifixion shows his love for humanity.
https://www.pexels.com/photo/crucifix-illustration-208216/

After facing the shame and wrath of crucifixion, Jesus was buried. However, just as prophecies of old revealed in Psalm 16:10, "For you will not abandon my soul in Sheol, or let your Holy One see corruption," Jesus rose again. This also confirms His words to His disciples when He told them in Mark 9:31 that "The Son of Man is going to be delivered into the hands of men. They will kill Him, and after three days He will rise". Jesus rose from the grave on the third day, defying death and ushering in a new life for all who believed. His triumph over the grave and death brought about hope and unspeakable joy to all who believed in Him.

The crucifixion and resurrection of Jesus first show His sacrificial love. Just as He said in John 15:13, "There is no greater love than this: that a person would lay down his life for the sake of his friends." This shows a love that goes beyond culture and time. The brutality of the crucifixion of the cross shows the weight of your sins and the great lengths Christ was willing to go to have you reconciled back to Him. The understanding of His sacrifice sheds more light on a Christian's hope beyond the challenges of life for an afterlife in eternity. This serves as the cornerstone of the Christian Faith.

Moments of Reflection

1. The Parable of the Prodigal Son is a powerful story of forgiveness and redemption. Is there any area of your life that makes you feel inadequate, imperfect, and detached from God, just like the Prodigal Son? What steps should you take following this parable?

2. From the parable of the Good Samaritan, who do you consider your neighbors to be, and is there anyone you need to extend a hand of compassion to today?

3. Do you believe that Jesus' life, death, and resurrection were for you? How can this reality affect your relationship with Him?

4. Jesus often emphasizes the importance of faith. Are you trusting God for something in your life right now? What actions are you willing to take to demonstrate your faith?

Exhausting the lessons of Jesus' life in a few pages would be impossible. To discover the many lessons and insights from the life of Jesus, His birth, miracles, teachings, trials, betrayal, cross, death, burial, and resurrection, you are encouraged to take on a personal in-depth study. Take your time studying the stories to unveil the truths and lessons they carry for your life. This is not an account of history but an invitation to the *more* that lies between the verses of the Bible – for a chance to experience a life of unending love and total victory found in Christ.

Chapter 5: Acts of the Apostles: The Early Church in Action

The story of the Apostles in the book of Acts follows the life of ordinary folks going about their daily activities but somehow encountering the most transformative experience that causes a noteworthy change in their lives and the world. They weren't superheroes or mystical beings but simply men living life: fishermen, carpenters, tax collectors, tent makers, etc. The change they had was due to the encounter they had with Jesus Christ after His resurrection. His arrival ushered in a new life for them that turned the world around. These were men like you, who started with uncertainty but chose to be guided by an unwavering faith in the One who called them and in whom they believed.

The change the Apostles had was due to the encounter they had with Jesus Christ.
https://www.pexels.com/photo/man-and-people-in-jesus-christ-and-apostles-costumes-8958075/

A spectrum of human expressions and emotions is revealed in this book when tracing key events in the lives of the Apostles: from faith to fear and back to faith again, joy, hope, and even moments of greed and anger. In essence, they were humans with normal human emotions but touched by the hand of God. The beauty of this book lies in God's seamless ability to make something great out of nothing. This chapter is meant to show you the hope that lies in yielding completely to God and encourage you to stay steadfast on the path while proclaiming the good news you have also received.

The Book of Acts Introduced

The book of Acts is attributed to the esteemed Apostle Luke, who also authored a Gospel named after him. It is recognized as a seamless continuation of his detailed narrative of the life of Christ. St. Luke the Evangelist penned the Acts of the Apostles in Greek, beginning from Christ's birth and extending through the early days of the Church. It is recorded that this book was composed between 70 CE and 90 CE and serves as a comprehensive account of the unfolding events within the burgeoning Christian community.

His style and manner of writing, seen in the Book of Acts, can be ascribed to his occupation. His care for the most minute things and his attention to detail transcended his role as a physician. It was seen in how he meticulously gave a detailed account of the early Church: the receiving of the Holy Spirit, the spread of the Gospel, Paul's conversion, etc. He was learned, and that added advantage helped him, through the inspiration of the Holy Spirit, to encapsulate even the experiences of others when he wasn't present at the happenings. Luke was believed to be of Greek descent, with some historians suggesting the possibility of him originating from Antioch in Syria, a province under Rome. However, both claims remain unclear. What remains unequivocal is that Luke's presence in Antioch resulted in a close companionship with Paul throughout his extensive missionary journeys. In one of Paul's letters, found in the book of Colossians, he affectionately addresses Luke as "the beloved physician." While Luke doesn't explicitly mention Paul by name, his use of the inclusive "We" in certain sections of the book of Acts strongly implies his direct participation in several pivotal events alongside Paul. Finishing what he started was important to him, as you will see in Acts 1:1-2, where he clearly stated to the recipient of the book of Acts, a man called Theophilus, that it was only right, that after talking about the life of Jesus, from his birth to the day He was taking up, he also discussed the lives and roles of the early apostles in the spread of the Gospel. He was able to achieve that to a great degree, as he provided a well-researched record of events surrounding the growth of the early Christian community.

The presence of the Acts of the Apostles in the New Testament is vital for the full comprehension of the message it carries. The transition from Christ's coming and how His disciples took up. It shows the series of events from Christ's ascension to the coming of the Holy Spirit in the upper room; how people left in doubt, worry, and fear after Christ's death were filled with boldness and power at the coming of the Holy Spirit. Not having this as a part of the compendium of the New Testament would have made the entire book impossible to understand.

Pentecost: The Coming of Fire and Power

The Pentecost was initially a celebration of the Jews; it was a time when they were expected to gather with their families and rejoice before Jehovah, their God. They were to observe this celebration with a free-will offering in their hands to Jehovah. It was a one-day feast, which took place fifty days after the Passover. It was observed regularly by the Jews, with many pilgrims trooping in from all around to take part. Pentecost originated from the Greek word "fiftieth," traditionally referred to as the Harvest feast or the Feast of Weeks, and took on new meaning for believers in Acts chapter 2. Beyond its original significance, it is now seen as the birthday of the Christian Church, marking the transformative arrival of the Holy Spirit.

> "When the day of Pentecost arrived, they were all together in one place. Suddenly, a sound came from heaven like a mighty rushing wind, and it filled the entire house where they were sitting. Also, they received divided tongues as fire appeared to them and rested on each one of them. And they were all filled with the Holy Spirit and began to speak in other tongues as the Spirit gave them utterance." (Acts 2:1-4)

This event, as recorded in Acts 2, was a fulfillment of the prophecy given to prophet Joel in Joel 2:28-32 concerning Pentecost. This fulfillment of the prophecy becomes one of the reasons why Jesus asked them to wait a while in Jerusalem before going out to proclaim the gospel.

> "And it shall come to pass afterward, that I will pour out my Spirit on all flesh; your sons and your daughters shall prophesy, your old men shall dream dreams, and your young men shall see visions. Even on the male and female servants in those days, I will pour out my Spirit. "And I will show wonders in the heavens and on the earth, blood and fire and columns of smoke. The sun shall be turned to darkness, and the moon to blood, before the great and awesome day of the LORD comes. And it shall come to pass that everyone who calls on the name of the LORD shall

be saved. For in Mount Zion and Jerusalem, there shall be those who escape, as the LORD has said, and among the survivors shall be those whom the LORD calls." (Joel 2:28-32)

The event sets Christianity apart and is a unique and beautiful style of worship. It is considered superior to other religions because of a promise fulfilled—the presence of the Holy Spirit among the believers.

After the resurrection of Jesus, He did not ascend immediately. He stayed a while, talking to His disciples and strengthening their faith. In the midst of that, their hearts were stirred up to go out and preach the gospel, but the power and boldness they needed to confidently declare the good news was not yet with them, and this power was Jesus' promise to them, that they would receive only if they waited in Jerusalem. So far, from the Old Testament to the first four books in the New Testament, records of the Spirit of God have only been mentioned to rest upon the men in whom He found favor and not within them. However, this method of receiving the Holy Spirit totally changed. The disciples, following Jesus's instructions, waited in Jerusalem for ten days, a testament to their strong faith despite the absence of Jesus. This was remarkable, considering the fear they must have felt after their leader's brutal death. Instead of fleeing, a logical choice at the time, they stayed and waited. The outcome was the outpouring of God's Spirit on all present in the upper room.

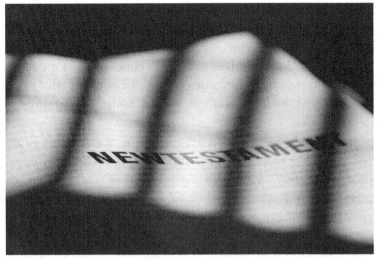

In the first four books in the New Testament, records of the Spirit of God have only been mentioned to rest upon the men in whom He found favor and not within them.
https://www.pexels.com/photo/newtestament-book-2565227/

On the day of the Pentecostal ceremony, the apostles were all together praying. The Bible describes the coming of the Holy Spirit as a sound from heaven like that of a mighty wind rushing in one direction and filling up the space they were in, followed by the appearance of what was described as "Cloven tongues of fire" resting on each person present. Something even more strange and magnificent was the aftermath of the sound and fire. The disciples, with the help of the Holy Spirit, spoke in the languages of the different people present during the feast of harvest as a confirmation of His presence in them. What adds to the grandeur is that pilgrims gathered during the Pentecost, representing diverse languages. Despite this diversity, the disciples were heard by all in their respective languages. Some of the persons present thought the disciples to be drunk, but Peter, Jesus' disciple, who was once shy, now filled with so much confidence, boldly refuted their claim and confidently began to preach to all present. He spoke of how Jesus of Nazareth, whom they had crucified, is their foretold Messiah and the living Christ, the One who had conquered sin and death and is now seated victoriously on the right-hand side of God.

The People became remorseful, repented of their past deeds, and inquired of Peter what they should do. Peter led them to full repentance by telling them how they were to turn from their wicked ways, repent wholeheartedly, believe, and receive Jesus Christ as their Lord and personal savior. On that day, about three thousand were recorded to be saved and became a part of the body of Christ by the power of the Holy Spirit. Peter's teaching that day is considered one of the most important and powerful sermons in the whole of the New Testament. That moment ignited a fire that resulted in the spread of the Gospel among the Jews and beyond to the Gentiles.

Great significance lies in the study of the event on Pentecost, from the meaning of the loud sound heard from heaven to the flaming fire and its choice in shape, even to the utterance they received. However, two key significances that must be highlighted are the fulfillment of God's promise, which showed that God always keeps His word, and no matter how long it takes, we are encouraged to wait because it will surely come to pass, as seen in Habakkuk 2:3. The second would be the importance of the coming of the Holy Spirit. God did not send His Spirit to have you sitting down; He imbues men with power by His Spirit to do His will seamlessly. This is evident with Apostle Peter and the other Apostles, who cowered in fear a while ago, having received the Holy Spirit, and became bold enough to lead three thousand souls to salvation in a day. After the outpouring of God's Spirit, the apostles and all other followers of Jesus actively continued in the propagation and proclamation of the good news, which is God's love for the world.

The Spread of the Gospel among the Apostles

The event at Pentecost led to a new expression of God's kingdom, so profound that it had most of the Jews of old completely sold out on the Gospel. It is a common occurrence to miss out on keywords and phrases as one studies the Bible, but keen attention must be paid to each word. This helps to provide a balanced understanding of what the Holy Spirit is trying to teach in that verse. At the start of Acts 3, a word was intentionally used, "Now" in certain translations and "One day" in others. This word or phrase showed a transition, a change, a highlight, or a marker indicating that something different from the norm was about to take place or had taken place, and you are now just witnessing the results of that change. This right here is noteworthy because it shows men who were regular fishermen and tent makers beginning to do things that will leave others in awe of God.

This helps to provide a balanced understanding of what the Holy Spirit is trying to teach in that verse.

The story says that Peter and John, on their way to the temple just as they had done in the past, came upon a man who was lame from birth and was begging for alms at the gate (known as "the Beautiful Gate") of the temple. Although this was not the first time they had seen this man, their encounter with the Holy Spirit would make all their experiences going forward novel and unique. Raising his hands, he sought alms from them, but this time, Peter had better help to offer the lame man – Jesus. Peter clearly stated that he had neither silver nor gold on him, but what he did have, he would give to him, and calling on the name of Jesus, he commands the lame man to rise and walk. On that very day, the lame man received both spiritual and physical healing. There is so much to learn from this singular story that applies to your life today. Often, the wants you so desperately crave can become a thick cloud, blinding you from the all-encompassing power of God. The lame man only had his sights set on the gold he could receive and almost missed the possibility that he could receive both spiritual and physical liberation.

From that "Now" in the first verse of Acts 3, the spread of the Gospel was like a dam breaking loose, taking up all that was on its path. The Bible records that more and more people believed, and multiple signs were given by God through the hands of the Apostles in Acts chapter 5.

> "The apostles performed many signs and wonders among the people. And all the believers used to meet together in Solomon's Colonnade. No one else dared join the apostles, even though they were highly regarded by the people. Nevertheless, as time went on, more and more men and women believed in the Lord and were added to their number. As a result, people brought the sick into the streets and laid them on beds and mats so that at least Peter's shadow might fall on some of them as he passed by. Crowds gathered also from the towns around Jerusalem, bringing their sick and those tormented by impure spirits, and all of them were healed." Acts 5:12-16 (New International Version).

The Persecution of the Early Church and Their Challenges

With the rise and spread of the gospel came profound challenges. In Acts 8, you are introduced to the great persecution that was committed against the believers in Jerusalem. They were about to have their fair share of trials and tribulations, just as Jesus had pre-informed them.

Right from the time of Jesus, the religious authorities of old, the Pharisees and Sadducees, have posed a strong opposition to the spread of the gospel. Seeing Jesus and his followers as a threat to their authority and leadership, they strongly fought against the advancement of the gospel.

Before the killings came, the opposition started as threats, which led to imprisonment. Before Peter and John were imprisoned, they were warned by the authorities not to preach the gospel, speak, or teach in the name of Jesus, which fueled them to declare Christ even more boldly. With the help of the Holy Spirit in them, they did not cower in fear, and God performed something marvelous for them in the prison. An Angel came that night, released them, and encouraged them to go into the temple and boldly declare the gospel, which astounded the sect of Sadducees. The persecution escalated quickly with the arrest of Stephen, one of the seven chosen for ministry. He was accused of blasphemy and stoned to death, becoming the first martyr of the early Church. Steven, who was stoned for the things he had said, became a trailblazer for future persecutions. Although the arrest of Peter and John after the healing of the lame man is the first record of the opposition the Church faced, it did not get heated until chapters 7 and 8.

The persecution they faced and how they handled it further emphasizes the importance of the apostles waiting for the outpouring of the Holy Spirit. Rather than serve as a damper, the persecution became a catalyst that greatly fueled the spread of the gospel all over Judaea and into parts of Rome.

The persecution and killing of Steven were led by a man called Saul of Tarsus, whom you will later know as Apostle Paul. His transformation from an avid persecutor to an active follower is one worth discussing. Following his leading in the persecution of Steven, Saul began a campaign against anyone who was a follower of Jesus, leaving the believers scrabbling in his wake as he entered into their homes and dragged them out to prison. He was quickly becoming a thorn in the side of the Church, but he had no idea how great the plans God had for him were. On his way to Damascus, after receiving information that there were believers gathered there, he had an encounter that would change his life forever.

While on his way with two other companions, a bright light shines down on them, and he encounters Jesus, which marks his turning point to becoming one of the most revered apostles of the early Church and to date. There is so much to glean from Paul's experience; the drastic change must not have been easy for him. At the start of his work with God, he must have felt lonely because most of the believers had yet to trust him. However, being completely changed, he seized the opportunity to have a relationship with his old crew. Aside from that, moving on from the guilt of the atrocities he committed in his time of ignorance would not have been an easy step.

Even with the conversion of Paul, the challenges continued, but for every challenge, the spread of the gospel soared higher. The opposition came from both the Jewish communities and the Gentile community, which raised internal issues between the Jewish believers and the Gentile converts. Members of the Jewish believers considered the spread of the gospel to the Gentiles wrong. They would not want to associate with them, and some of the apostles, like Peter, also held this belief. It took a vision from God to change his view on that. Peter believed that before redemption would be extended to the Gentile community, they would first have to be converted and become Jews. God revealed to him in a vision that none of the things created by Him can be considered unclean when He, God, had not done so. In the vision, God instructed Peter to kill and eat various beasts, and Peter would not because he considered them unclean. He had the same vision three times before coming to understand what it meant: that God accepted any man who would fear God and work in righteousness and that such man should be accepted by him as well. It was after this that Paul came to him, and Peter was able to accept him in Acts 10.

The lesson here is not to be a judge but to love and receive everything and everyone with the love of God. This newfound understanding would help bridge the gap and aid in the propagation of the gospel all over the world.

It is easy to get lost in the praises of Paul and miss seeing him as a mere human, helped by God. He had many struggles but was able to overcome them all by the power of God at work in him. When you go through life's challenges, you must know that your situation is not unique to you and, most importantly, that the power of God is available to help you get through and come out stronger. Remember, just like Apostle Paul, you are not alone.

The baptizing of Saint Paul.
https://www.flickr.com/photos/paullew/7203069100

Moment of Reflection

1. The Day of Pentecost is a pivotal moment in Acts, marked by the outpouring of the Holy Spirit. What are your thoughts on the role of the Holy Spirit in your life today?

2. The book of Acts portrays the early Christian community as sharing everything in common. Reflect on the concept of communal living and generosity. How might this principle be applied around you today?

3. The conversion of Saul (later Paul) is a significant turning point in Acts. Have you ever experienced a transformative moment in your beliefs or values? How did it impact your perspective and actions?

4. The missionary journeys of Paul and other apostles highlight the spread of Christianity to diverse cultures. How do you feel about sharing your newfound faith with others?

5. Acts recount several instances of miraculous healings. If you could perform a healing miracle, what ailment or condition would you choose to address, and why?

6. Reflect on the concept of resilience in the face of persecution, as seen in the lives of early Christians in Acts. How can their

experiences inspire your perseverance in challenging circumstances?

7. Peter's vision addresses his questions on the inclusion of Gentiles into the Christian faith. Reflect on moments in your life when you have had to navigate and reconcile differences in beliefs or practices with others.

The story of the early Church shows a union of divine intervention and human determination, which resulted in explosive results. See yourself today through the lens of the early Church and each Apostle talked about in the book of Acts. There are no limitations when you choose to walk and work hand in hand with the Holy Spirit; the results are beyond anything you could ever fathom. The significance of the book of Acts emphasizes the peace, joy, and confidence that Matthew 19:26 brings when it says, "...With God all things are possible!"

Chapter 6: Paul's Letters: Foundations of Christian Doctrine

Paul was referred to by some as the Apostle of Progress; his life was truly progressive in the way in which the world views growth today. Like many, he didn't get it right the first time, but eventually, he did. Paul progressed in ways that have left many and still leave many in awe. Only a few of Jesus' twelve apostles could equal the impact Paul had. This isn't to downplay their roles and efforts in the establishment and advancement of the early Church; they did very important work. However, Paul gave Christians the gift of his epistles on which the early and modern Church foundations are laid. These foundations still hold firm today because of the sacrifices of a man who thought it all as gain to ensure the spread of the good news beyond the borders of Judea.

St. Paul.

Who is Paul, and what makes the life of this messenger of grace so profound? You are about to get these questions answered, as this chapter is solely dedicated to his background, occupation, service, conversion, trials, missionary journeys, teachings, letters, and ministry in general.

The Early Life of Apostle Paul

Paul, over time, was known as many things: an Apostle, a spiritual pioneer, a critical thinker, Saint Paul, the teacher of the Gentiles, etc. However, before these names existed, he was just *Saul of Tarsus*, a tent maker by trade, a Pharisee by upbringing, and a zealous persecutor of the early Christians.

Saul was recorded as being born in Tarsus, a vibrant city east of Cilicia. Just as with other prominent figures of old, there are discrepancies in the exact location of his birth. Others believed he was born in a town in Galilee called Giscala and later relocated to Tarsus with his parents in the early years of his life. Ascertaining the exact date of his birth has not been possible, but there have been attempts based on gathered information. Since he was referred to as a young man during the persecution of Steven in the Book of Acts and was active in his missionary journeys during the 40s and 50s, it was inferred that he must have been born around the time of Jesus, which is 4 BCE, or a little later. His time of death is also estimated to be around 62-64 CE.

Growing up in Tarsus held a lot of significance in Paul's later years. Tarsus was a prominent town and a province ruled by the Romans, which resulted in its rich cultural diversity. Paul's background as a Roman citizen and a tent maker shaped his ability to adapt to multiple cultures and gave him a sound educational background. This helped him bridge the gap between the Jews and the Gentiles for the gospel's sake during the fulfillment of his ministry. His Jewish education was obtained under the tutelage of Gamaliel, a Pharisee and a highly esteemed Jewish rabbi of his time. He also gained proficiency in other essential areas, like being bilingual and learning the craft of tent making, which provided him with practical and essential skills at that time, as well as financial support during his many missionary journeys.

Paul's Transformation: Adversary to Ally

Paul's conversion from a Pharisee to a major antagonist of the teachings of Pharisaism, a youth from a strongly heathen city to a major critic of all their practices, and a born Hebrew to a strong contender against the Judaic exclusiveness was a miracle.

Paul grew up to attain a high level of strictness, which he used in his approach to the persecution of the early Church. This was due to his educational upbringing by a well-renowned Jewish teacher, which was in perfect accordance with the laws of his fathers. Because of their rigorous adherence to the Mosaic laws, the Jews are known as one of the strictest sects. Still known as Saul of Tarsus in the early chapters of Acts, Paul's devotion to Pharisaism is seen in his zeal towards the persecution of the early Church. He fervently opposed what he considered to be a deviation from Judaism. In the eighth and ninth chapters, it was revealed how far he was willing to go to uphold his beliefs. In Acts 8:1-3 and Acts 9:1-2, Paul's role was significant in the punishment given to all who chose to follow Jesus, consenting at one point to the stoning of Stephen, the very first Christian martyr. In his own words, as you would later read in 1 Timothy 1:13, he describes himself at this time of his life as a persecutor, blasphemer, and insolent man. However, all these versions of him were about to change for the better.

In 1 Timothy 1:13, he describes himself at this time of his life as a persecutor, blasphemer, and insolent man.

His victory in conquering and persecuting the Church fueled his ambitions. It raised his stakes when he persecuted Christians from other towns and cities. This pushed him to travel down to Damascus from Jerusalem in the hope of finding followers of Christ there. It was on this very journey that his conversion took place; he was said to be "arrested by God." As Saul journeyed with his companions, having received a letter from the High priest permitting him to persecute the Christians of the Damascus synagogue, he experienced the most transformative moment of his life. During the encounter, a bright light shone down from heaven upon him, and he heard a voice, as seen in Acts 9:4-6

> *"And he fell to the earth, and heard a voice saying unto him, 'Saul, Saul, why persecutest thou me?' And he said, 'Who art thou, Lord?' And the Lord said, 'I am Jesus whom thou persecutest: it is hard for thee to kick against the pricks.' And he, trembling and astonished, said, 'Lord, what wilt thou have me to do?' And the Lord said unto him, 'Arise, and go into the city, and it shall be told thee what thou must do.'"*

The intensity of the encounter blinded him, and he was supported for the rest of the journey to Damascus. While he was there, he remained blind for three days, and he neither ate nor drank. In those moments, God was instructing one of his servants, Ananias, to go to Paul and help him restore his sight, and Ananias, knowing Paul's reputation, was hesitant. Nonetheless, he went in full obedience to God's instructions. Coming into Paul's house, he healed, baptized, and filled him with the Holy Spirit, which marked his birthing into the Christian faith. Following his conversion, Paul didn't delay; he was immediately seen declaring Jesus as Christ in the synagogue. Many found it hard to believe that the leading man in the persecution of the Church, who had come down to Damascus for that very reason, was now advocating for the very cause he had fought against.

Although many were astonished, others, like the Jewish leaders, were not pleased and sought to kill him. Being aware of the threat to his life, he escaped in a basket through an opening in the city wall with the help of the disciples present. From then on, he stepped into a new chapter in his life, one completely devoted to the spread of the gospel, and with a change in his name from Saul to Paul. This new phase in Paul's life stands as a stark contrast to the pre-transformed Saul, which shows the profound impact of his encounter with the risen Christ on the road to Damascus. This transition from persecutor to Apostle highlights the transformative power of Grace and redemption in Paul's journey.

Paul's Epistles

In the many epistles written by the Apostle Paul, you can perceive his literary prowess. However, the ability to take down his epistles was less attributed to his expertise in writing and more to the Holy Spirit's divine work through him. Paul's Letters, being foundational to the New Testament, shaped Christian theology.

Here is a detailed overview of these letters and their purpose;

Romans: Unveiling the Foundations of Faith

The Book of Romans was originally written for the Christian Church in Rome and, by extension, also for modern Christians today. Outside its powerful message, its clear, comprehensible, concise, and systemic style of presenting the Christian doctrine makes it a quick favorite of young or new Christians. At the beginning of a new Christian's Bible study, Romans always make it on the list of first reads.

The Apostle Paul wrote the Epistle to the Romans to address several key theological and pastoral concerns within the Christian community in Rome. He addressed topics ranging from the believers' justification by faith and the righteousness of God to the world's need for salvation. The theological richness that Romans possess makes it a cornerstone of the Christian doctrine. At the time Apostle Paul wrote this Letter to the Roman Church, the Christian community in Rome consisted of both Jews and Gentiles. It is not news that there was discrimination towards the Gentiles by the Jewish Christians. In his letter, he emphasized the importance of unity and mutual understanding among them while highlighting their shared salvation through faith in Christ Jesus in Romans 15:5-7. It is very easy for strife to come in between relationships when you are not being watchful, even for the most minute reasons. It could be between your spouse, sibling, friend, child, or co-worker. etc., but you are encouraged by Paul always to remember that you are to receive each person just the same way Christ received you.

1st and 2nd Corinthians: Wisdom and Guidance for the Church

Similar to Romans' advocacy for unity and oneness, the books of Corinthians addressed the Church in Corinth, a major city in Greece. It is one of the key books in the New Testament that focuses on a single union within God's body. Corinth, being a city that served as the center of Greek culture, was a commercial city teeming with people from all around the world, meaning this was reflected in the total population of the Church. The diverse nature of the Church meant disagreements were almost inevitable, and love and harmony became the second most discussed topic after immorality for the Corinth Christians.

The subject of morality was also a major one for the Corinthian Church, and they struggled greatly with it. Raised in the heart of Greece with its pagan ways, where sexual rites are common occurrences at every feast and ceremony, and words like chastity and monogamy were novel, these new Christians found it difficult to uphold morality. So, Apostle Paul saw the need to put more effort into addressing it. Besides Paul's address of these two topics, he also talked about other things, such as the misuse of spiritual gifts. He gave guidance on such topics as marriage and the Lord's supper in the first part of Corinthians. The second part of this book is concerned with Paul's defense of his apostleship, discussing what the true nature of a Christian ministry should look like and encouraging followers to live in light of the new covenant. Generally, a central theme for both books is an address on the balance of grace and discipline among a diverse Christian community.

Galatians: Freedom in Christ's Grace

Apostle Paul leads the Galatian Church through a series of teachings and exhortations in his letter to them. Addressed to them at Galatia, his letter was centered on the theme of Grace as he vehemently opposed any form of legalistic teaching making its way into their Church. In this letter, he aimed to show them their complete sufficiency of faith in Christ for their Salvation, clearing them of any form of doubt that they needed the law, that is, the Jewish tenets, to guarantee their justification in Christ.

Key themes in Galatians are the justification of faith, freedom in Christ, and crucifixion with Christ. In Galatians 6:14, Paul informs the Church of Galatia, "But far be it from me to boast except in the cross of our Lord Jesus Christ, by which the world has been crucified to me, and I to the world." Here, he talks to them about being identified in Christ's death and resurrection and how this union with Christ transforms the Christian life. Another profound scripture on the topic of justification of faith is Galatians 2:16:

"Yet we know that a person is not justified by works of the law but through faith in Jesus Christ, so we also have believed in Christ Jesus, to be justified by faith in Christ and not by works of the law, because by works of the law, no one will be justified."

This scripture teaches you that justification can only come through one source, which is faith in Christ; any other attempt by one's effort will prove futile. Trying to earn salvation on your terms and by your effort shows you are undermining the finished work of Christ. This is said while not undermining the place of spiritual discipline.

Ephesians: The Unity of the Body in Christ

While on his third missionary journey, Apostle Paul was in the City of Ephesus for more than two years, where he ministered to the people there. Being a city that housed the Greek goddess Artemi's temple, many opposed his ministry for different reasons. Still, many were also converted to the faith. After he left, he was imprisoned for the first time, and it is believed that it was there that he wrote the Ephesians Epistle along with other letters to the Philippians, Colossians, and Philemon. The book of Ephesians took on a more formal approach. Whether because of its importance or his lesser acquaintance with the Church in Ephesus remains unknown.

In this letter, Paul talks about topics that are at the very core of a Christian's belief in both faith and practice. He addressed topics on the mystery of God's will, unity in Christ, and spiritual warfare. Within the first three chapters of the letter, Paul talks about how God, through the gift of Grace in Jesus Christ's death and resurrection, created a special and holy community. In this community, He has specially chosen individuals whom He has adopted as His sons and daughters through Christ's accomplishments. Regardless of being a Jew or a Gentile, everyone who becomes a partaker of this grace was once dead spiritually because of their wrongdoings but has now been brought into life through the deeds of Christ alone.

While not attempting to address just a particular problem in their morals or theology, his focus was on avoiding future problems by getting the followers of the Ephesian Church to grow in their faith and become mature Christians. After elaborating on these profound theological truths in the first half of the book, Paul straightforwardly expressed his expectation: he envisioned that this community of Christians would embody its heavenly calling. So, by seeking to divide the letter into segments in his address, although not intentionally, the first part shows you the truth, and by applying the truth, the lifestyle talked about in the second part becomes possible to fulfill. Scriptural verses like Ephesians 1:9-10, Ephesians 4, Ephesians 6, etc., address these topics directly to give you a better understanding.

Philippians: Joy in Unity and Christ-likeness

The book of Philippians is one of the books in the New Testament, and it scores as a great hit among today's Christians due to its great and easily relatable verses. All books of the Bible have their fair share of popular verses, but Philippians have a host of them. A verse like Philippians 1:6, which says, *"He who began a good work in you will carry it on to completion until the day of Christ."* conveys hope beautifully; it serves as a reassurance when you feel overwhelmed or on the verge of giving up.

Another one of such great verses that stir up faith within you is Philippians 4:13, which says, *"I can do all things through him who strengthens me."* This verse gives you the boldness and confidence to go through the hardest of challenges, the confidence not in your ability but in the excellent power of God. A third one is, *"For me to live is Christ and to die is gain."* as seen in Philippians 1:21. This statement by Paul shows you the insignificance of this world without the purpose of fulfilling Christ and the reward of a better life to come after this world.

However, originally written to the Church in Philippi while Paul was in prison, these verses are loved and appreciated by the Church and were written to address key themes like joy in all circumstances, unity and humility, pressing toward Christlikeness, and the surpassing worth of knowing Christ. He radiates a theme of joy amidst challenging circumstances. When in prison, he expresses gratitude for the Church's partnership in the gospel and shares profound insights on Christian living.

Colossians: Embracing the Fullness of Christ's Supremacy

The Epistle to the Colossians, likely written by Paul during his imprisonment in Rome (around AD 60-62), unveils the profound teachings regarding the supremacy of Christ. This letter, addressed to the Church in Colossae, is a powerful exposition on the all-sufficiency of Christ in matters of faith and Salvation. The Colossae church was believed to have been established during his third missionary journey by one of his converts, a Colossian visiting Ephesus, Epaphras. In response to the good news he had heard from Paul, he returned to his city to share it with them. This scenario was like the story of the Samaritan woman who came in contact with Jesus in John 4:5-30 and yielded the same result.

This scenario was like the story of the Samaritan woman who came in contact with Jesus in John 4:5-30 and yielded the same result.
https://commons.wikimedia.org/wiki/File:Lavinia_Fontana_Christ_and_the_Samaritan_Woman_at_the_Well.jpg

The first reaction after receiving the gospel with joy is always to share it. As a Christian, proof of the word of God being implanted in your heart is in your desire and zeal to share it with others. Although Paul never had the opportunity to visit the Colossian Church, through his interface with Epaphras, he is made aware of the struggles faced in the Church, and he wasted no time in addressing them head-on. He wrote the Colossian Epistle after finding out that the supremacy of Christ's rule as the head of the Church and as the son of God was being demeaned by some false teachers.

The Church at Colossae was under attack from false teachers who were denigrating the deity of Jesus; they were teaching that He was not actually God. Paul addressed these issues by emphasizing the preeminence of Christ in creation, redemption, and the reconciliation of all things, urging Christians to acknowledge and embrace His comprehensive supremacy, as you would see in, Colossians 1:15-20, *"He is the image of the invisible God, the firstborn of all creation... For in him all the fullness of God was pleased to dwell."*

He also discussed other subjects, like finding complete fullness in God and living life totally in Him. He warned them not to consider other notions like deceptive philosophies and human traditions and to embrace virtues like compassion, kindness, humility, patience, and gentleness in Christ.

1st and 2nd Thessalonians: Embracing Hope, Holy Living, and End-Times Expectation

The letters to the Thessalonians, probably written by Paul in the early 50s AD, focused on the anticipation of Christ's return, the importance of living a holy life, and guides what to expect in the end times. However, intended for the Christians at Thessalonica, these epistles offer encouragement, practical advice, and insights into what to expect in the future. Its core message is on the anticipation and hope a Christian should have concerning Christ's second coming. He addresses their concerns when they inquire about the fate of a departed Christian by teaching them in depth the events that surround Christ's second coming and practical Holy Christian living, a quiet life, excelling in love, and working diligently.

A scripture that can quickly make it onto your list of favorites is 1 Thessalonians 5:16-18. Paul states, "Rejoice always, pray without ceasing, give thanks in all circumstances; for this is the will of God in Christ Jesus for you." It is a soothing and encouraging charge, one that can bring about peace and calm when you hold on to it wholeheartedly.

Other Epistles: Navigating the Pauline Wisdom and Pastoral Counsel

The remaining book collection of Pauline Epistles, comprising Timothy, Titus, Philemon, and Hebrews, adds the extra finesse needed by Christians for a well-grounded understanding of the way of life for the new era of Christianity. Some of these letters may not have been written by Paul directly, but they are in line with his teachings. They address multiple themes, from topics on leadership and Christian conduct to your relationship with God and Christ's supremacy. Although some of these subjects have been touched on in the previous books, these last epistles lay a much-needed emphasis on them again for your sake. For example, the book of Hebrews dedicates ample chapters to talking about the supremacy of Christ, providing crucial insights into the topic of the new covenant and the significance of faith.

Moments of Reflection

1. Is there a change in your view of salvation based on Apostle Paul's teaching of justification by faith?
2. How can you contribute to fostering unity within your local Christian community?
3. Reflect on Paul's metaphor of the body. How does it shape your view of diversity within the Church?
4. What spiritual gifts do you believe God has given you, and how can you use them to serve others?
5. How does Paul's description of love in Corinthians 13 inspire your relationships with others?
6. Reflect on a time when you experienced comfort from God. How dis it impact your faith?
7. In which areas of your life do you need to pursue reconciliation, following Paul's teachings?
8. How does recognizing the supremacy of Christ influence your perspective on life's challenges?
9. Reflecting on your identity in Christ, how does it shape your self-worth and purpose?
10. In challenging circumstances, how can you maintain a spirit of joy, as encouraged by Paul?
11. Reflect on the role of gratitude in your life and its connection to joy.

In what way can you cultivate humility in your interactions with others? How does Paul's model of servant leadership challenge your common perceptions of leadership?

The life of the Apostle Paul stands as a testament to the transformative power of God's grace. His journey from a zealous persecutor to a devoted follower of Christ reflects the profound impact of encountering Jesus Christ. Paul's epistles, filled with theological depth and practical wisdom, continue to guide and inspire Christians today. As you navigate the pages of his letters, you will find a road map for living out the Christian faith with authenticity, love, and a steadfast hope in the promises of Christ. The enduring legacy of Paul extends beyond the 1st-century churches, resonating with believers of every era, inviting them to embrace the grace that transforms lives and to walk in the light of Christ's redemptive love.

Chapter 7: Revelations

Many are curious about the future and will do anything to have a glimpse of what it holds. This desire is not exactly wrong, as it's a part of a human being's general make-up. God doesn't want you to be ignorant about the things He wants you to do, and if you find yourself not in God's plan, it's because you haven't aligned completely with Him. This can be verified all through the Bible, where you see God reveal His will and plans to His servants who are in total service to Him. Some of these things are yet to happen, but He made them open and public to anyone who cares or is interested in knowing what will happen in the future. In books like Daniel, Ezekiel, Isaiah, Joel, Zechariah, and the major one dedicated to this cause, Revelation, you will see prophecies made about what is to come at the end of the world and the fate of the followers of Christ.

God reveals his plans in the book of Revelation.

God has revealed His plans to His faithful servants so that they may share them with His children. Although the relevance or significance of this book is not limited to just that, neither is it primarily about the future. There is so much more that can be harnessed from the book of Revelation, and an understanding of this will help you grow and improve your knowledge of God and His will for you.

Revelation Introduced

The book of Revelation is derived from the Greek word "Apokalypsis," which means "Unveiling" or "Revelation." Unlike the Old Testament, the Book of Revelation is the only apocalyptic book in the New Testament. This book is one of the most challenging for Christians due to the vivid imagery and symbolism contained in it. Many would rather read any other book of the Bible than Revelation. Having an understanding of this book through an overview will help you see the weight of the message contained in it and build your interest in grasping every lesson you can get by reading the entire book. A greater challenge than its comprehension is its application. You have to be willing to make key adjustments in the areas pointed out by the writer. However, it is worth noting that with this great challenge comes great blessings.

In the past, the book of Revelation was generally accepted to be under the authorship of the great Apostle John, who also wrote the books the Gospel of John and 1st, 2nd, and 3rd John, meaning he wasn't new to penning down experiences and sharing his knowledge and walk with God in writing. It is deduced that his role as an apostle of the early Church, with a lot of influence, was the reason why he did not see the need to add a title, as the people to whom he wrote were well acquainted with him, and his name alone was enough introduction. These and more were the basis by which earlier scholars accepted Apostle John, popularly known as "John the Beloved," as the author of this book.

In recent times, there has been a great variation in thoughts and ideas towards the authorship of the book of Revelation. Modern-day scholars and theologians state that just a name alone given within this book is not enough to certify that John the Beloved actually wrote it, and all that is known of the author is that he was a Christian prophet. They claim it could have been any John who ministered back then. They also claim there's a difference in the writing styles used in the Gospel of John and the other books (1st, 2nd, and 3rd Books of John) and that of the book of Revelation. Other scholars who believed that John the Beloved wrote Revelation have rebuffed this argument, stating that the genres of both books are different, and this can affect the writing style used. They also claim that anyone in the state he was when the book was written, on the Aegean Island of Patmos, located off the west coast of Asia Minor, would write differently and that he also lacked the advanced scholarly items used for writing as of that time and could not possibly have had access to them on that island.

Modern scholars still stand firmly on their beliefs that it could be any John – and the evidence provided for Apostle John's case is not solid enough to make a definite decision that he authored this book. With this understanding, they have resolved to always refer to the Author of Revelation as simply "John of Patmos" or "John the Elder" to achieve a common ground.

Historical Context

Revelation, written in 96 CE, was a time in John's life when the Romans ruled over large parts of major continents like Africa, Europe, and Asia, where the churches John was addressing were situated. This very factor had a major significance in John's address. At a time when the majority of Asians were apathetic towards Christian doctrines, some remained steadfast in the apostles' doctrine. This did not go well with the then Roman Emperor, Nero, who commanded the execution of all Christians, and this decree was likely to be emulated by the Emperor, Domitian, who was leaning towards the persecution of the Church as well, as they would not bow and worship him like all others. This was a highly crucial time for the Christians, as the advocation for Emperor worship was on the rise. It is also worth noting that this very factor was the reason John was on the Island of Patmos. He was exiled there for preaching the gospel and declaring Jesus as Lord.

Emperor Nero commanded the execution of all Christians.
cjh1452000, CC0, via Wikimedia Commons. https://commons.wikimedia.org/wiki/File:Nero-black.png

The Apocalyptic Genre of Revelation

The book of Revelation adopted a unique writing style called an apocalyptic genre, commonly found within Jewish and Christian texts. Similar to prophecy, apocalyptic literature communicates revelations from visions and dreams. It is often a combination of elements of reality and fantasy. Books like Daniel also share similar themes and literary devices. Deciphering the core message was likely more effortless for the initial recipients at that time than for today's readers who are unfamiliar with this literary style. Individuals of that era were used to this writing style because it was prevalent. As a modern reader, you will have to adopt an "ancient eyes" perspective, which involves understanding the literary conventions of that time and the historical events that prompted the utilization of such a distinctive style. That is, the only way to have a rich understanding of an apocalyptic book is to view it through a lens that reflects the mindset of its original audience.

The Letters to the Seven Churches: Unveiling Divine Insights

In the book of Revelation, letters were addressed to the seven churches, and each letter combines symbolic language with vivid imagery to provide timeless significance and relevance in today's world. This book, although written by John, was written in full obedience to Jesus Christ's instructions. He was instructed to write to the seven Asian churches, namely, Ephesus, Smyrna, Pergamum, Thyatira, Sardis, Philadelphia, and Laodicea, to warn and encourage them as they underwent different struggles, both internal problems, like laxity & morality, and external challenges, such as persecution and execution from the Roman empire. Following the introduction and instructions, we see John's address to these seven churches in the 2nd and 3rd chapters. Each Church receives a message with its letter that addresses their unique struggles and how to make adjustments.

At the start of the first vision in Revelation 1:20, John sees seven candlesticks, like that seen by Zechariah in Zechariah 4:2. The candles represent the seven churches he would be addressing. A candlestick is a good depiction of the Church, which is meant to represent the light in this dark world and shows its role in helping others receive the light. The candlestick, where seven stars were said to represent the Angels, was believed to be the church leaders back then. For all seven churches, the template was the same when writing their letters, but the content differed. It always begins by commending the Church, followed by words of encouragement, then reproof, and ends with counsel on how to return from their errors, and finally, a promise of hope on what they stand to gain by being faithful. The message to the Church wasn't just to the Church alone, but to all those struggling to stand firm on their choice in service to God.

The Loveless Church: Letter to the Church in Ephesus

The Ephesian Church is a story of returning to one's first love. In the letter, Jesus urges them to remember, repent, and then return. This is a complete process, one that is also expected of every Christian today. The letter to the Church in Ephesus was written in the time of the early Church when the apostles were still alive, and the city was in its prime. Being a city with a vibrant metropolis made it the center for trade and commerce and a hub for Greek spiritual activity, as it was a city dedicated to the Greek goddess Artemis.

John began the letter to the Ephesus with praises for their tireless zeal and unrelenting dedication to the growth and spread of the gospel. It is worth noting that Jesus, in the vision to John, didn't just begin with reproof; he commended their good work. This shows that total service to God isn't just commendable; it's worth emulating. Serving God and watching Him change the lives of others through you is deeply satisfying. Their refusal and distaste of the teachings and actions of some groups back then – ones that didn't mind engaging in immoral acts as long as it hurt no one – was another plus for the Ephesian Church (and one for which they were commended). This group, called the "Nicolaitans" didn't think it necessary to put a stop to the desires of the flesh. They thought it all alright to act as they liked, engaging in the pleasures of the flesh, while they still claimed to be in service to God. They tried to share this opinion with the rest of the body of the Church, but the Ephesians would not cave in. However, they got caught up in their desire to serve God, and they lost sight of their hearts until they were no longer driven by their love for Jesus.

This raises the question, how does one stay busy for Jesus without loving him? Well, you saw it with the Church in Ephesus. The Bible doesn't say what their motivation was; there could have been a host of reasons, but one possibility is religiosity, meaning being busy just for the sake of it. This goes to show that it's possible to not love God and serve in His house, but it is impossible to love God and not serve in His house. This is a crucial revaluation that all Christians should take regularly. Ask yourself, "Is my heart right with God? Do I do the things I do out of love for Him or because of religion?" For the Ephesians, their actions were not the problem; Jesus was more focused on their motivation. What fueled the things they did?

The Ephesus church had grown cold in heart, and their service to Him had become ritualistic. Here, Jesus provides counsel on what to do. He says that they should remember what it was like when they had just found Him and how vibrant, fiery, and alive their hearts were for Him, and then urges them to repent. It is one thing to remember and realize your faults and wrongdoings, but it is a completely different thing to be willing to change and chart a new course for yourself, regardless of how far gone you are. Aside from the reproof and counsel, He also lets them know that there would always be a repercussion for their actions and what would happen if they were not quick to change. He, however, did not leave them trembling at the thought of the consequences of their actions but offered them hope as well, via a promise. He assured them there was a tree of life of which they would eat and an eternal paradise awaiting them; this would keep them in high spirits as they worked towards change.

A beautiful thing worth noting about God's method is that after He highlights the problem to you patiently, He doesn't leave you alone to figure out how to go about it. He takes further steps by explaining its consequences and how they can greatly affect you and then leaves you to make an informed decision without pressure because He has given us the ability of free will.

The Persecuted Church: Letter to the Church in Smyrna

The Church in Smyrna, also called the suffering church, is a perfect example of beauty from ashes. When faced with the toughest of persecutions, rather than being crushed by it, it served as a stepping stone for them to ride upon and show forth the glory of God. This letter to Smyrna was one of comfort and assurance to those who were in troubling times. Jesus began by saying to them, "I know." This was a reassurance for them that they were not alone, that He saw their struggles, and that in due time, He would bring them out stronger and better. For the Church in Smyrna, unlike the others, there was no reproof; that wasn't what they needed; rather, the words spoken to them at that time were words of encouragement.

To better understand the state this Church was in, it's believed that the leader presiding over the Church was a man called Polycarp, who in the height of Roman worship, was burned at the stake because he refused to pledge allegiance to the Roman Emperor and swear his loyalty by offering incense. It didn't stop there; Emperors like Marcus Aurelius, Vespasian, and Domitian, in their relentless pursuit, would have them placed in extremely shabby prisons, dragged into the arenas in rags, burned, killed and fed to the wild beasts of the field. Jesus then comforts them by encouraging them to be faithful and assures them of His knowledge of their situation and His presence with them. Although they faced intense persecution, this Church did not give in to the ways of the Romans. They thought it worthwhile to endure the pain and hardship in the name of Jesus Christ, hoping to obtain an incorruptible crown in the end. A thought-provoking conclusion is that the Church with the strongest persecutions turns out to be the purest. Holding fast to God's word in the face of adversity is the best approach to sailing through.

The Compromising Church: Letter to the Church in Pergamos

Unlike the Ephesian Church, the Church in Pergamos gave ears to the ways of the Nicolaitans, and they began to drift away from the word of God and found themselves giving in to the ways of their environment. They went after wealth and luxury at the expense of their work with God. It wasn't that they didn't love God; they were made to believe that they could love God and love their present world, too, and no one has to suffer. However, Jesus came very direct in His message of repentance to them. He gave them the same counsel as Ephesus: repent, return, and change.

The Corrupt Church: Letter to the Church in Thyatira

Just as in His message to the loveless Church, Jesus began with commendations for their efforts in getting better, acknowledging their deeds, love, faith, service, and perseverance. After this, Jesus dives right into the reproof; although there was no mention of the Nicolaitans, the Thyatira church was said to engage in their approved practices, which the Christian faith disapproves. Beyond being a place of trade, Thyatira was also a place of war, and this made it difficult for the people to get by. The only known way of survival for them was being a part of the trade guild, which was of huge importance to civic society at that time. The guilds were known to eat the meals offered to idols and engage in other idolatrous acts. This became a problem for the Christians. Jesus encourages them to let go of their idolatrous ways and turn to Him. He lets them know the consequences of not listening to Him. Also, He tells them about the promise made to those who heed His words; to those who overcome, He would give authority over the nations and many more things.

The Dead Church: Letter to the Church in Sardis

The letter written to this Church was written at a time when there was a deep fallout of Christians in the early Church, but even with this, there remained those who upheld the light of the gospel. The Sardinian Church was a church with a false show of righteousness; they made promises without fulfillment, and their outward display of strength showed careless confidence and want in their watchfulness. The message to the Church in Sardis was not really one of condemnation but more of disapproval. They were called hypocrites who made a show of a burning passion for the things of God but were actually dead inside. Jesus talks about not finding their works perfect, meaning they made an effort to work, but that was only to put up a front that they still had everything put together. Jesus would rather they acknowledge they have lost their way, retrace their steps, go back, and start again than act like they are still on the right track.

The Sardis church fell at a time when the Church seemed to be living in its past glory; they had come to a halt and were stalling but refused to acknowledge and address the problem. They had grown content in resting on their past victor's laurels.

The Faithful Church: Letter to the Church in Philadelphia

The city of Philadelphia was a major Grecian town because its main purpose was to spread and promote the unity of customs, spirits, and loyalty for the sake of the empire. It was very successful in its pursuit of the empire. This means there was a strong practice of the Grecian way in Philadelphia, but regardless, the Church remained faithful. Jesus commends them greatly when He said they possessed little strength but did a lot and didn't give in at any moment to the ways and systems of their present society. There were no reproofs for this Church, but he made many heartwarming promises. He promised them an open door, which no man would ever be able to close, and a show of His power over those who opposed them.

The letter to the Church of Philadelphia challenges today's Christians. Jesus mentioned that with what little strength they had, they persevered, meaning you're never to say you're without help or strength. You should also trust in the depth of God's love to help you in every circumstance.

The Lukewarm Church: Letter to the Church in Laodiceans

As you would see in your study of this Church, they seemed to be the worst of the bunch. There were no commendations given to them by Jesus. He rather dived right into their problems and His reproof of their attitude. He began again with the same phrase used in His address to the other churches, "I know." This shows that there truly is nothing that can be hidden from the sight of God; He sees right into the deepest thoughts of your heart. This Church was in a worse state because it was hard to find them anywhere, just as Jesus described them to be neither cold nor hot. This statement meant they did not openly accept Jesus, nor did they openly reject Him, and made the house of God seem like a social club where they gathered to have fun.

For this reason, Jesus said He would spit them out of His mouth. Following the reproof, Jesus still acknowledged them as the ones He loves, urging them to repent. This shows just how much God loves His Children, that even in their filth, His love still shines through, calling them out into His light.

The letter to the seven churches, although written to actual locations in the 1st century, carries a great spiritual significance today. It addresses the state of hearts that exists within the Church. When you examine yourself thoroughly and with all honesty, you will find areas of your life aligning with one or more of the cases of the churches in Asia Minor. So, it's advised that you deeply study these letters, the reproofs, corrections, and counsels to shape your life better.

The Other Visions

In the Book of Revelation, the shift from the letters to the seven churches reveals a vivid picture of events and symbols: seven seals being opened, seven trumpets sounding, and seven bowls pouring out God's wrath. This apocalyptic tale has sparked various interpretations, with Christians and scholars grappling over what these visions truly mean. One widely accepted view suggests that these symbols represent a spiritual struggle between good and evil. The seven seals, trumpets, and bowls are seen as metaphors for an ongoing battle throughout history — a clash between the forces of goodness and malevolence. This perspective argues that these visions depict the enduring fight between God's plan for salvation and disruptive forces trying to thwart it. Key figures, like the Antichrist and the two witnesses, are often seen as symbolic representations rather than literal individuals.

The seven seals, trumpets, and bowls are seen as metaphors for an ongoing battle throughout history — a clash between the forces of goodness and malevolence.

Rodhullandemu, CC BY-SA 4.0 <https://creativecommons.org/licenses/by-sa/4.0>, via Wikimedia Commons.
https://commons.wikimedia.org/wiki/File:15_Angel_with_long_trumpet_window,_St_Nicholas,_Halewood.jpg

On the flip side, some interpret these visions more literally, proposing specific historical and future events. The seals, trumpets, and bowls are thought to be concrete predictions of wars, natural disasters, and divine judgments in a specific chronological order. This perspective views the imagery as a kind of road map for understanding God's divine plan as it unfolds over time. The identity of the Antichrist and the interpretation of the final battle between good and evil becomes a central point of contention. Some argue that these are symbolic representations of societal and spiritual conflicts.

In contrast, others insist on a more straightforward reading, pointing to specific historical figures or future individuals embodying these roles. This disagreement sparks heated debates over the timing and nature of these apocalyptic events. The role of the two witnesses is another puzzle, with interpretations ranging from symbolic representations of God's faithful messengers to claims of their literal presence during a future period of tribulation. This diversity in perspectives reflects the complexity of Revelation's imagery and the challenge of making sense of symbolic language in connection with historical or future occurrences.

Debates also arose over the timeline of these events. Some believe in a futurist interpretation, suggesting that most of Revelation's prophecies are to unfold in a specific end-time scenario. Others take a historicist perspective, connecting the visions to events throughout history. Meanwhile, preterists argue that many of the prophecies were fulfilled in the early centuries of the Christian era. In the unfolding narrative of Revelation, different angles of interpretation come together, creating a complex and intricate understanding of these apocalyptic visions. The challenge lies in navigating the tension between symbolic and literal readings, accepting diverse perspectives while seeking to grasp the underlying messages that transcend time and cultural contexts. As Christians and scholars continue exploring Revelation, the rich and varied nature of its imagery ensures that debates over its meaning will persist, offering a fertile ground for theological exploration and reflection.

Moments of Reflection

1. Explore the historical tidbits shared about early Christian communities. How might understanding the context enhance your appreciation of Revelation's messages?

2. What are your thoughts on the messages of hope and salvation woven throughout the narrative, and how do these themes resonate with your spiritual journey?

3. How has your perspective on the book evolved, and what questions or mysteries still linger in your mind?

4. Think about the relevance of Revelation's messages in today's world. How might its themes of justice, redemption, and divine intervention speak to issues and challenges today?

5. Consider the role of faith and perseverance in the face of adversity, as depicted in Revelation within the Church in Smyrna. How do you draw strength from these themes in your own life?

6. Ponder the idea of Revelation as both a warning and a comfort. How do you balance the urgency of its message with the assurance of God's ultimate victory?

Beyond the disagreements that arise from trying to understand this book, for the Christian, there is so much knowledge and insight to be drawn from its pages. Rather than trying to follow the debates, focus more on the light within its pages that offers you a chance at a better Christian journey. The exploration of the book of Revelation is not a one-time deal; its message endures, meaning a revisit often, is necessary. You should employ continuous study and reflection on its lessons.

Chapter 8: Old Testament Prophets: Voices of Warning and Hope

The prophets within the books of the Old Testament can be pictured as messengers chosen by God to communicate directly with Him. Their role in the stories of God's chosen people is profound, offering you a window into a world of guidance, warnings, and hope in diverse situations. They can also be envisioned as ancient heroes, standing up for what's right in a world filled with challenges. As you look into the Bible, there's hardly a key event of that time not tied to their influence.

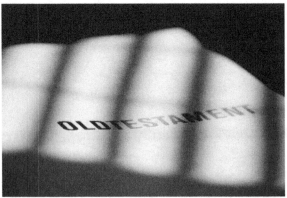

The prophets within the books of the Old Testament can be pictured as messengers chosen by God to communicate directly with Him.

Explore the stories of these messengers, the crucial messages they conveyed to the people of ancient Israel, and the impact they had, not only in their time but in the lasting relevance of their teachings today. As you navigate the intricate nature of their experiences, consider how their words and messages can serve as beacons of insight in your own life.

A Prophet and His Role

A prophet is someone who interacts with God on behalf of His people. Prophets in the Old Testament were figures who spoke on behalf of God, warning the Israelites about their sins and calling them to repentance; they played an integral role in communicating God's will and purpose during a time of political crises. Their messages were not always the same or conveyed in the same manner; some messages can be more dramatic than others. Certain prophets, like Zechariah and Ezekiel, were able to see elaborate visions. Some played the roles of a mediator or a judge. In contrast, others, like Malachi and Torah, dedicated their lives to working to mend the people's relationship with God, constantly urging them to remember the allegiance they made with the God of Israel and the Torah, which means the Law. Only those who fell under these rules are regarded as prophets.

In some cases in the Old Testament, certain persons spoke or wrote prophetic statements. Still, these people are not considered prophets of the Old Testament. Such a person would be Saul, the first king of Israel, in 1 Samuel 10:9-12, who, under the influence of God's Spirit, prophesied, although what he prophesied about was not recorded in the Bible. However, he prophesied, but the role he played in the Story of Israel is not a prophetic one as he was not called to be a prophet. For this reason, the Bible does not count him as a prophet.

The Major Prophets

The major prophets were significant figures who played pivotal roles during a tumultuous time in Israel's history. They proclaimed a consistent message, warning God's people about the consequences of disobedience while offering a future hope of restoration. Their words provided a sobering reminder for all generations of the importance of staying faithful to God's covenant. At the same time, they broadcast God's steadfast love and promise of new life on the other side of judgment. The fact that you get to study these ancient prophets' messages shows their timeless relevance.

Isaiah: The Messianic Prophet

Isaiah, a key prophet among the Israelites, emerged as a learned voice expressing crucial topics in the divine plan of God. He was an advocate for righteousness, truth, and unwavering faith in God in his teachings, which was during the time of Israel's turbulent monarchy. His book, which is named after him, Isaiah, now stands as the epitome of prophetic writing. The prophet's mention of the "Suffering Servant" evidently teaches about Christ's role as the servant and the agonies that will come with His mission. Isaiah goes beyond writing about events; he charged against moral downfall and worship of idols and called for repentance and heeding to the Word of God. Despite these warnings, he still gives out flickers of hope, persuasively telling people that the path of goodness is the way out to God. The prophetic visions by Isaiah rose above the social, political, and religious context of his time to explore the universal themes of justice, mercy, and the transcendent nature of the divine-human relationship.

His role as one of the prophets of the Old Testament remained influential even in the New Testament, which confirmed the fulfillment of his prophecies on Jesus Christ. Holy writers and Apostles specifically drew parallels with Isaiah's thoughts, which reaffirms his critical place in our comprehension of the messianic role of Jesus Christ.

Jeremiah: The Weeping Prophet

Jeremiah, a towering major prophet, becomes a strong voice in the Old Testament, profoundly shaping the divine narrative. The importance of his work is manifested far above the scope of his book in his principle to get the message that carries elements of warning, lamentation, and hope across. In Israel's history, Jeremiah's prophetic ministry unfolded amid political crises, invasion, and exile. As Jerusalem faced tragic exile, Jeremiah perceived its gravity, recognizing the city's portrayal of profound suffering.

The book of Jeremiah has diverse themes, such as favor and punishment from the Lord, repentance, and the restoration of people from captivity. It explains how the world is not a place where individuals can do whatever they want, the reality of judgment, and a hope of revival. Jeremiah's prophecies were more symbolic, like when he used a potter's clay to illustrate how humans were predominantly under the control of the Almighty. Towards the end, loyal scribes received a critical message introducing the concept of a new covenant and a promising hope amid judgment chaos. Along with this covenant, God mentioned a time when His law would be engraved on hearts, symbolizing a definitive change from the heart.

Jeremiah ("the weeping prophet") has demonstrated his compassion for his people by preaching the hard message while also bearing personal sufferings. He was quite ready to bear the losses for the sake of the sacredness of his calling. Jeremiah's implication serves as a timeless reminder of moral and spiritual decay. The battles he fought, the tears he shed, and the hopes he clung to should remind you of the difficulties faced at different times in your life. Jeremiah transcends his time in the pages of the Old Testament and becomes a beacon symbolizing eternal truth. His poems are filled with discoveries about faith and reveal his thoughts about God, reflecting human life.

Ezekiel: The Visionary Prophet

Ezekiel, one of the major prophets in the Old Testament, is a tremendously striking and assertive persona that no one can ignore. Considering the length of his book, Ezekiel, as the messenger of God in the Old Testament, preached a mixture of visual images, spiritual insight, and a call for divine obedience. In the time of the Babylonians' exile, Ezekiel had a grueling job of preaching to the audience, who were worn out and incarcerated. The portrayal of prophetic visions in his works, sometimes fantastical and symbolic, conveyed divine messages that surpassed the immediacy of the context. The prophetic visions of the prophets were often messages from God that went beyond that current time. Ezekiel's role was, however, not limited to warnings of future events. He served as a mentor, spurring the people to be more repentant and renew their faith in the Lord.

The Book of Ezekiel, among others, manifests in prophecies, visions, and symbolic activities. It deals with godly rerun, revitalization, and God's power in world affairs. The Prophet Ezekiel, in the passage about the valley of the dry bones, artistically points out that, even in seemingly hopeless situations, there is a possibility of spiritual renewal and resurrection. Not only does Ezekiel provide a unique and imaginative vision of the restored temple, but this vision also represents the fact that the divine presence of God is once again among the people. This vision was a light on the path ahead, manifesting a trust that God was steadfastly pursuing His covenant despite the tribulations of exile.

EZEKIEL 48:28

28 'The southern boundary of Gad will run south from Tamar to the waters of Meribah Kadesh, then along the Wadi of Egypt to the Mediterranean Sea.
29 'This is the land you are to allot as an inheritance to the tribes of Israel, and these will be their portions,' declares the Sovereign LORD.

The gates of the new city
30 'These will be the exits of the city: beginning on the north side, which is 4,500 cubits long, 31 the gates of the city will be named after the tribes of Israel. The three gates on the north side will be the gate of Reuben, the gate of Judah and the gate of Levi.
32 'On the east side, which is 4,500 cubits long, will be three gates: the gate of Joseph, the gate of Benjamin and the gate of Dan.

The Book of Ezekiel.

Ezekiel, a watchman whose reverence for his mission is unmatched, is unshakable in his commitment. He was always determined to deliver his messages, even when confronted with opposition. Today, his messages, just like the others, continue to ring true, serving as a timeless reproach for those who have grown complacent in their spiritual lives and offering reassurance through divine reinstatement and hope. His book is a reflection of his experience, character, and guidance that is still useful in finding oneself and inner peace today.

Daniel: The Interpreter of Dreams

Daniel, a figure of distinction among the major prophets, emerged as a beacon of faith and resilience in the Old Testament. His significance goes beyond the length of his book, showing his unwavering commitment to God amid challenging circumstances. During the Babylonian exile, Daniel's life in the royal court shows him facing trials and temptations. His steadfast devotion to God and refusal to compromise his principles, as seen in the story of the lion's den, exemplifies his unwavering faith. The Book of Daniel is a mix of prophecies, dreams, and historical accounts. Daniel's interpretation of King Nebuchadnezzar's dream and the subsequent visions offers profound insights into God's divine plan. The prophetic passages, including the vision of the four beasts and the seventy weeks, glimpses into future events with remarkable precision.

The debate surrounding Daniel's classification as a major prophet adds complexity to his legacy. While in many Christian traditions, Daniel is considered a major prophet, the Hebrew Bible often places him among the writers rather than the prophets. His life exemplifies resilience in the face of adversity. From his early days in Babylon to encounters with powerful rulers, he consistently relies on God's guidance. His unwavering trust is encapsulated in the well-known story of the fiery furnace, where he and his companions emerge unscathed, which is a testament to God's divine protection.

In a contemporary context, his life encourages Christians to stand firm in their faith, even in challenging situations. His experiences remain timeless lessons on integrity, prayer, and trust in God's providence.

The Minor Prophets

The Minor Prophets, a collection of twelve concise yet powerful books in the Old Testament, constitute a diverse and often overlooked segment of biblical prophecy. Unlike the major prophets, whose extensive writings dominate the prophetic landscape, the minor prophets offer profound insights into compact narratives. These prophetic voices, Hosea, Joel, Amos, Obadiah, Jonah, Micah, Nahum, Habakkuk, Zephaniah, Haggai, Zechariah, and Malachi, collectively contribute to a rich form of messages that address diverse themes such as justice, repentance, and the coming redemption.

Spanning through different historical periods and addressing different audiences, the minor prophets convey divine messages with a concise yet impactful eloquence. Their writings delve into the intricate dynamics of God's covenant relationship with His people, revealing the consequences of disobedience and the enduring hope of restoration. Despite their brevity, the minor prophets played a significant role in the broader prophetic tradition, complementing the narratives of their major counterparts. Each prophet contributed a unique perspective, capturing the uniqueness of their respective historical contexts while conveying timeless truths that resonate with humanity's enduring struggles and aspirations.

As you explore the collective wisdom embedded in these brief yet potent books, you will get to unveil a beautiful picture of prophecies that speak to the intricate interplay between the sovereignty of God and human responsibility. These prophets, although considered minor due to the length of their books, were major contributors to the prophetic parts that echoed throughout the Old Testament and in today's world as well.

Hosea

Hosea, a minor prophet in the Old Testament, led a life that illustrated God's love and human frailty. God asked him to marry Gomer, a woman of unfaithfulness, meaning a harlot. Hosea's struggles mirrored Israel's spiritual unfaithfulness to God. Despite Gomer's infidelity, Hosea's unwavering commitment became a living metaphor for God's enduring love towards a nation known for its perpetual unfaithfulness. Hosea's prophetic ministry extended beyond his marital metaphor. His messages, often accompanied by visions, emphasized the consequences of Israel's spiritual adultery and called for repentance. The prophet's life exemplified God's redemptive yearning, culminating in the symbolic act of purchasing Gomer back after her descent into slavery.

In the face of personal heartbreak, Hosea's obedience conveyed a timeless message of God's relentless pursuit of His people. His life stands as a constant testimony to the transformative power of God's love, urging all to heed the call to repentance and embrace the enduring grace of God's faithfulness.

Joel

Joel, as a minor prophet, was a voice of significance in the Old Testament. He delivered a concise yet powerful message centered on repentance, God's judgment, and restoration. Although very little is known about his personal life, the timelessness of his message extends beyond the pages of his book. Joel's focus on the day of the Lord and future judgment was illustrated with a locust plague, and in urging repentance amidst calamity, he emphasizes the importance of turning to God. He envisioned a restoration of God's blessings upon genuine repentance, revealing God as a merciful and gracious deity. Despite the brevity of his book, Joel emerges as a significant voice, urging his audience to recognize the profound consequences of their actions and embrace the promise of divine restoration through heartfelt repentance.

Amos

Amos, a shepherd-turned-prophet, arises as a formidable voice among the minor prophets in the Old Testament. This is due to the grand content of his messages, regardless of the size of the book. His messages, delivered during a period of affluence and moral decay in Israel, condemn social injustice and religious hypocrisy. Amos boldly proclaims God's judgment against nations, including Israel, emphasizing that true worship extends beyond the rituals they practiced and has more to do with justice and righteousness. Despite his humble beginnings, Amos confronted kings and priests without fear, denouncing exploitation and calling for repentance. His visions, including the plumb line and the basket of ripe fruit, vividly illustrate impending judgment. Amos's enduring relevance lies in his uncompromising call for social equality and genuine devotion, challenging Christians to align their actions with God's standards of justice and righteousness.

Obadiah

Obadiah, although being the shortest book in the Old Testament, is loved by many Christians. Its concise nature and deep message resonate with the Christian life. Popular verses like Obadiah 1:17, "But upon mount Zion shall be deliverance, and there shall be holiness, and the house of Jacob shall possess their possessions." are often used today. This book presents a profound message through its minor prophet. In addressing the nation of Edom, Obadiah delivers a stern warning about impending judgment due to their pride, violence, and betrayal towards their brother nation, Israel. The prophet unveils a vision of Edom's downfall, emphasizing divine retribution for their arrogance and mistreatment of Israel during times of distress.

Despite Edom's lofty mountain strongholds, Obadiah prophesies their ultimate humiliation. This short yet impactful book serves as a stark reminder that pride and injustice will not go unnoticed by a just and sovereign God. Obadiah's message goes beyond the specific historical context, urging everyone to reflect on the consequences of arrogance and cruelty while highlighting God's commitment to justice and the protection of His people.

Jonah

The life of Jonah, as humorous as it is, is full of lessons. Jonah tried outsmarting God out of fear, like so many today, trying to act smart to get God to bend His will or plan for one reason or another – for Jonah, it was fear. He was instructed by God to prophesy against the city of Nineveh but attempted to escape this divine calling. In the process, God trapped him in the belly of a fish, where he repented, and when he was released, he fulfilled God's command. Jonah's story emphasizes God's compassion for repentant hearts when He forgave the people of Nineveh due to their genuinely remorseful response following Jonah's message. The prophet's initial reluctance and God's patient correction reveal a broader message about God's universal concern for everyone.

Jonah's unique narrative serves as a compelling reminder of God's grace. It challenges Christians to embrace His mercy and extend it to others beyond personal biases and prejudices.

Micah

Micah, one of the minor prophets of the Old Testament, delivers a powerful message that focuses on themes of justice, humility, and hope. He was born in a rural setting and grew up to become a strong voice against corruption and oppression in both Samaria and Jerusalem. His prophecies condemn social injustice, exposing the mistreatment of the poor and vulnerable. Micah foresees a future where God's justice prevails, and peace emanates from Zion. His famous words, "Act justly, love mercy, and walk humbly with your God," capture the essence of his prophetic message. Micah's vision extends beyond his time, urging nations to pursue righteousness and recognize the enduring hope found in God's redemptive plan, ultimately pointing toward the arrival of the Messiah in Bethlehem, as foretold by this humble shepherd-prophet.

Nahum

Nahum is regarded as a prophet of doom and deliverance. He emerged as a powerful voice among the minor prophets in the Old Testament. His focus was on the impending judgment against Nineveh, the capital of the Assyrian Empire. Nahum vividly describes the city's imminent downfall, portraying God as both a jealous avenger and a refuge for those who trust in Him. The Prophet's striking imagery includes clear depictions of nature's forces and divine retribution, emphasizing the consequences of Nineveh's oppressive reign. Nahum's message, delivered with poetic intensity, reassures the oppressed and warns the oppressors. Despite its seemingly harsh tone, Nahum's prophecy showed the balance between divine justice and compassion, revealing God's commitment to justice and the protection of His people in the face of ruthless tyranny.

Habakkuk

Habakkuk engages in a unique dialogue with God, addressing the perplexities of injustice and divine response. His story and life happened in a time of societal turmoil. Habakkuk questions God's apparent silence in the face of wickedness. In a profound exchange, God unveils His plan, assuring that justice will prevail. This shows that as a Christian, you can always talk to God and be sure that He will respond. Habakkuk's journey from doubt to trust was shown in his powerful prayer and affirmation of faith. The Prophet's name means "embrace" or "wrestle," symbolizing his intimate struggle with God. Despite the uncertainty, Habakkuk emerges with an unwavering trust in God's sovereignty, proclaiming that, even in the absence of visible prosperity, he will rejoice in the Lord. Habakkuk's dialogue exemplifies the authenticity of wrestling with faith and finding strength in surrender to God's unfathomable wisdom and providence.

Zephaniah

Zephaniah, a prophet during Josiah's reign, delivers a powerful message against Judah's corruption. Connected to Hezekiah, he rebukes societal sins, warning of God's imminent judgment. The prophet vividly describes the "Day of the Lord," urging repentance. Just like Obadiah, he condemns arrogance and pride, emphasizing humility. Amid stern warnings, he foretells a remnant finding refuge in God, which offers a glimpse of hope. His poetic expressions capture the judgment's severity and the promise of restoration. Beyond the immediate context, Zephaniah anticipates ultimate redemption through the Messiah. In a morally decayed era, Zephaniah challenges individuals to seek righteousness, humility, and a genuine relationship with God. His timeless words call for repentance and refuge in the Lord's mercy.

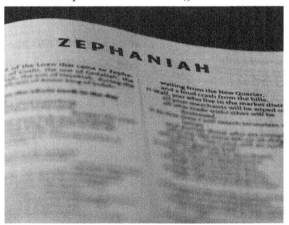

The Book of Zephaniah.
https://www.pexels.com/search/Zephaniah/

Haggai

Another favorite of many is the book of Haggai. Haggai was a post-exilic prophet, but despite this, he emerged as a focused messenger with a message to rebuild the ruined temple of Jerusalem. He spoke about the people's neglect of the house of their God amid their surpluses and abundance. Haggai then called for a renewed commitment to reconstruct the temple, linking national blessings to obedience. He emphasized the importance of prioritizing God's dwelling place while promising divine favor upon their efforts. His strategic leadership plays a crucial role in motivating Zerubbabel, the governor, and Joshua, the high priest, to resume temple construction despite challenges.

Through Haggai's exhortations, the people rekindled their commitment to God's house. The completion of the second temple attests to Haggai's impact and symbolizes the restoration of worship and divine presence.

Zechariah

Zechariah, also a post-exilic prophet, collaborates with Haggai to inspire the reconstruction of the temple in Jerusalem. His prophecies, delivered in symbolic visions and clear oracles, cover a broad spectrum of themes, including the restoration of Jerusalem, the coming Messiah, and the future kingdom of God. Zechariah's visionary messages blend encouragement with stern warnings, urging repentance and a return to God's ways. The prophet's emphasis on the dual roles of the coming Messiah, a humble servant and a conquering king, contributed to a rich Messianic imagery. He envisioned a purified and reunited Jerusalem, one that symbolized a future era of divine restoration.

Zechariah's prophecies, while deeply rooted in the post-exilic period, extend beyond that time, offering a panoramic view of God's redemptive plan. His words resonate with Christians, prompting reflection on God's faithfulness, the significance of repentance, and anticipation of the ultimate fulfillment of Messianic promises.

Malachi

Malachi, the concluding prophet of the Old Testament, addressed a post-exilic community that struggled with spiritual apathy and compromised worship. His name, meaning "my messenger," underscores his role as a divine messenger. Malachi confronts the people with God's enduring love and their unfaithfulness, challenging them to return to genuine worship. Through a series of dialogues, Malachi addresses issues like priestly corruption, marital infidelity, and offerings lacking sincerity. He anticipates the coming of a messenger preparing the way for the Lord and a prophetic nod to John the Baptist preceding Jesus. Malachi's messages revealed God's desire for heartfelt devotion and faithfulness. His prophecies echo themes of repentance, restoration, and divine intervention. His conclusion solidifies the Old Testament, emphasizing the importance of obedience and a faithful remnant. His words today urge Christians to examine their devotion and embrace the transformative power of God's enduring love.

Moment of Reflection

1. Consider the historical context of the prophetic books. In which ways do the societal challenges faced by the prophets mirror or differ from challenges in today's world?

2. Reflect on the role of repentance in the prophetic messages. How does the concept of turning back to God apply to your own life?

3. Explore the recurring themes of judgment and restoration in the prophetic books. How do these themes provide a framework for understanding God's interaction with His people?

4. Consider the Messianic prophecies found in the prophets. How do these prophecies shape your understanding of Jesus Christ and His significance?

5. Reflect on the messages of hope and redemption in the prophetic books. How can these messages inspire resilience and faith in the face of adversity?

6. Consider the relevance of the prophets' calls for social justice and care for the marginalized in today's society. How do these teachings affect your actions and attitudes?

7. Reflect on the personal journeys and struggles of the prophets. How do their experiences with God's call and correction relate to your spiritual journey?

8. Consider the overarching theme of God's faithfulness throughout the prophetic books. How does this theme impact your understanding of God's character and your relationship with Him?

It has been hundreds of years since these prophets lived and their books were written, but their words still hold deep truth today. That's the amazing thing about the Bible; it's a living, breathing book that continues to speak into the lives of those who would have it. As you read further into the books of the prophets, keep an open heart and mind, and ask God to reveal any area of your life that needs adjustment and transformation.

Chapter 9: The Historical Books: From Joshua to Esther

Other books of the Bible also address events that happened in the past, but these books you are about to read contain some of the most fascinating stories that shape a Christian's early life. They contain an array of events, ranging from shifts in leadership, kingdom divisions, royal reigns, exiles, triumphant returns, love stories, etc. This chapter will guide you through all these events by simplifying the tales and bringing life into the characters and their impact on a Christian's faith. You mustn't approach these books as another history text or an enjoyable fictional novel, but rather as a detailed account of the lives of people who once walked on this earth, having real feelings and emotions and their crosses and burdens to bear. They were regular men and women just like you, with real-life challenges and temptations, flaws, and weaknesses. Still, they chose to yield and surrender their wills to God, even in seasons when it seemed impossible. They are reflections of human courage, faith, and divine intervention. As you move through these pages, open your heart to receive wisdom and inspiration for your life.

They were regular men and women just like you, with real-life challenges and temptations, flaws, and weaknesses.

What Are These Books About?

These historical books are more than just people, places, and events; they embody broader themes that resonate with other parts of the Bible. Five major themes can be drawn from them: God's sovereignty, presence, promises, kingdom, and covenant. Here is a more detailed look into each theme:

1. **God's Sovereignty:** The historical books consistently portray God as sovereign over all, from nature to the affairs of nations. His authority is demonstrated through miracles and requires Israel's submission.

2. **God's Presence:** Throughout these books, God was intimately involved in the affairs of men. He appointed leaders like Joshua, judges in times of distress, and chose kings. His closeness is evident in the assistance provided to godly kings and prophets. Yet, at times, his presence seems obscured, often linked to Israel's sin or, in some cases, a deliberate act.

3. **God's Promises:** The historical books, especially those echoing the themes of the Pentateuch (Five Books), leave no doubt that Abraham carried the promise and that the promise outlived him. This promise – called the "Abrahamic Covenant" – constituted of land possession, children proliferation, and blessing, was primarily fulfilled in Joshua's time.

4. **God's Covenant:** The Abrahamic Covenant implied that conformity to the Lord's commandments was a very serious human duty, demonstrated by the faithfulness of Abraham. Another covenant called the Mosaic Covenant will then arise to govern life per the past covenant that promised rewards for righteousness and punishment for unrighteousness, which is frequently depicted in historical books.

5. **God's Kingdom:** The sovereign power of God is reflected explicitly in His rule over the world but also implicitly through earthly kings. They served as God's representatives on earth, entrusted with His kingdom, as depicted in texts like 2 Chronicles 13, Zech. 7:9 and 1 Chron. 29:5.

The Historical Books

Below are the books from Joshua to Esther:

Joshua

In the Book of Joshua, the seasoned leadership of Moses was replaced by the courageous leadership of Joshua. This section symbolizes a decisive point in human history, which was just before the Israelites entered the promised land to fight and claim their inheritance. The story opens with the death of Moses, the celebrated guide who led the Israelites through the desert. Now, the leadership role was given to

Joshua, a consecrated follower of Moses. The book of Joshua records the whole journey of the Israelites to Canaan, a land dedicated to them by God. The whole story is centered on the crossing of the Jordan River, a miraculous event depicting the parting of the Red Sea in the time of Moses, the fall of Jericho walls, and the sun remaining motionless at Joshua's command during a difficult battle. These deeds were the results of obedience and divine intervention in the wake of the Israelites, and they also signify God's presence with them. The book also describes some territories that were allotted to the twelve tribes in the process of settling in Canaan, which served as a blueprint for the Israelites. The address comes to a close with a solemn covenant established between the people and a faithful God.

The Book of Joshua depicts the importance of having unswerving faith and remaining faithful when dealing with God. The life of Joshua lays out the foundation for the other biblical accounts, reminding us of how legacy is built on trust in God and staying true to one's principles.

Judges

The Book of Judges comes up as a thrilling sequel to Joshua, detailing the turbulent times of the past in Israel. While employing the Promised Land as a narrative background, the book follows a sequence of chronicles from the moment of capture to the time of oppression and the cycle of actions and reactions, the time of the judges. While the Israelites settled into their designated areas, God appointed different judges, charismatic and dedicated people, to guide and lead them to freedom from oppression. These judges, such as Gideon, Samson, and Deborah, played a key role in the lives of the Israelites. The Book of Judges highlights the culture and politics of that time. It portrays a society dealing with the human complexities of being faithful. In their constant struggle for power amidst the ups and downs of their victories and defeats, the Israelites also deal with the problem of coexistence with neighboring people and the attraction of gods of other tribes. The entry of each judge is the resounding echo of the nation's call for liberation, portraying a manifestation of divine acts amid human imperfection.

The Book of Judges.

The cycle of rebellion, oppression, repentance, and miraculous intervention of God reveals the spiritual and moral tests suffered by the Israelites. The Book of Judges, beyond the historical collection, is a grand examination of human nature. It reveals the issues around the aspirations of a people endeavoring to stick to their covenant with God. It is a colorful picture of the typical human experience: flawed leadership, social turmoil, and the everlasting faithfulness of a forgiving God. This era of the judges paved the way for more profound discourses on the maze of divine-human relations and the endless quest for justice and righteousness. Some of these judges were:

- **Deborah:** Deborah, a prophetess and judge, defied societal norms with unwavering faith. Her wise counsel and leadership guided Israel to victory against the Canaanites. She is known for the pivotal role she played in securing Israel's freedom.
- **Samson:** Samson, marked by incredible strength and Nazirite vows, grappled with personal weaknesses. Despite his flaws, his exploits against the Philistines showcased God's power working through human frailty. His life revealed the consequences of succumbing to temptation.

- **Jephthah:** Jephthah rose from an outcast to a judge. His vow, resulting in his daughter's sacrifice, epitomized the complexities of devotion and the human cost of rash promises. His leadership secured a brief rest for Israel.
- **Gideon:** Gideon, initially doubtful, became a courageous leader. He led a small army to defeat the large Midianites army. His story highlights the transformative power of faith and God's ability to use unlikely individuals.
- **Ehud:** Ehud, a left-handed judge, orchestrated a daring assassination of Moab's oppressive King, Eglon. His strategic and decisive action liberated Israel from Moabite oppression, exemplifying God's unexpected deliverance.
- **Othniel:** Being Israel's first judge, he rose to prominence by defeating the Mesopotamians. His leadership set a precedent for the judges who followed because of his faithfulness to God. Othniel exemplified the importance of obedience in securing God's deliverance.

Ruth

The Book of Ruth shows God's faithfulness, salvation, and favor through the eyes of the main character, Ruth, after whom the book is named. The events in this book took place at a time when judges still governed God's people. That aside, it was also a troubling time for the Israelites as they faced intense agricultural problems. The story starts with Naomi's family leaving for the Moab lands because of a great famine that has already affected the lands of Israel. Tragedy strips Naomi of her spouse and sons, rendering her childless. Ruth, Naomi's daughter-in-law, decides to cling to her in her trying times when she declares, "The people you like should be my people, and the God you worship should be my God also." Ruth 1:16-17. Ruth and Naomi moved back to Bethlehem, struggling financially as widows and working on the gleaners' rows to survive. Ruth earns the admiration of Boaz, who later marries her and brings redemption to her mother-in-law.

Culturally, Ruth provides a glimpse into Israelite customs, kinship ties, and the practice of kinsman-redeemer responsibilities. The story reflects societal expectations, economic challenges, and the resilience of individuals navigating uncertain times. Also, Ruth's action suggests how a person's choice matters in the larger story of life, as well as destiny. The story is one of hope in God to make restitutions. The main theme is the combination of individual strife, societal actions, and the ever-present guidance of God.

1st and 2nd Samuel

The books of 1st and 2nd Samuel, which embody the historical narrative of ancient Israel time, document a complicated phase of evolution from the season of God being their only king to the establishment of earthly kingship. The main characters are Samuel, the last judge; Saul, a central prophet and Israel's first king; and David, the most important figure. David started as a shepherd boy and ended up as a king and an iconic person in Israel's history. The story began with the account of Samuel's birth and his subsequent selection as a messenger of God. However, amidst the people's request for the appointment of an earthly ruler, God instructs Samuel to anoint Saul as the first king of Israel.

Culturally, these books reveal Israelite religious practices, the society around them, and the family (clan) as the base of their life. It reveals the Jewish people's attempts to form a centralized governing structure while simultaneously confronting external threats and domestic fragmentation. The story depicts the disagreement between the tribal way of life and the rise of a new monarchy. It shows how the tribal culture was strengthened against any changes, especially those related to the governmental system. In the book, you will be shown the challenges that come with leadership and the outcomes of not obeying God's orders. Saul's reign is noted for its achievements and defeats, leading to a protracted process for him to secure his power and preserve the Israelite covenant. The ascent of David marks a new epoch in the history of Israel through bravery, craftiness, and favor of God.

Both books are highly linked to the Israelite's resilience toward political intrigues and spiritual rebirth. The tales of Samuel, Saul, and David are timeless stories that teach us about leadership, faithfulness, and God's power in a nation's affairs.

1st and 2nd Kings

The books of 1st and 2nd Kings are the history books that continued where the books of 1st and 2nd Samuel left off. These books handed out a detailed account of the monarchy period by presenting the kings' reigns and Elijah's and Elisha's prophetic ministries. This book gives its readers an overview of the political, cultural, and religious situations of ancient Israel. You will come across different kings of the kingdom of Israel and Judah whose performance is benchmarked by their obedience to the Lord's statutes.

Concerning culture, these books talk about Jewish religious practices, social codes, and their belief in one true God, which was often corrupted with idolatry. The general theme of these books was the continuous conflict the Kings of Israel had within themselves on total loyalty to God and their attraction to the foreign gods. One after the other, they faced the same struggles as they aimed to establish a covenant with God.

Both books provide a stark view of what happens if leaders happen to engage in wrongdoing. The storyline reflects the cycle of apostasy, God's wrath, and God's restoration of Israel. With a focus on royal succession and court politics, the books tackle the ideas of power, loyalty, and the lasting repercussions of men's actions. In the end, the books of the 1st and 2nd Kings deliver a cautionary teaching but at the same time testify to the sincerity of God, who remains faithful despite human imperfections.

1st and 2nd Chronicles

The first and second books of Chronicles provide a different story of the history of Israel from the Bible. These books deal with genealogies, culture, and the reigns of different kings, giving a detailed insight into the country. The 1st Chronicles is opened by genealogies covering the descendants from Adam to the Davidic line, and the promise of God is seen in the continuity of the chain. This is followed by a section devoted to the Davidic reign, where his pattern of kingship was described as one based on worship. Solomon's auspicious reign, which fulfilled the construction of the Temple, was the most prominent event, and it was elaborated extensively with a focus on all the religious rituals.

The Book of Chronicles 1.

Ceremonially, these books are focused on the importance of worship, the role of the priesthood, and the significance of God's law within the culture of faith. The First Book of Chronicles presents an idealized view of Israel's history, in which most of it emphasizes the spiritual aspects and the persistence of the covenant cords. The theological agenda of the chronicler (referring to the writer of the book) aspires to worship God wisely and stay loyal to the right person. In political terms, 1st and 2nd Chronicles replay the monarchy period, stressing the kingships of David and Solomon and continuing to trace the rulers of Judah. The chronicler passes his judgment on every monarch according to their devotion to the Lord and compliance with the covenant. The explanation reveals the theological interpretation of historical reality, emphasizing the political consequences of obedience and disobedience.

In summary, 1st and 2nd Chronicles are meant to be a theological reflection of Israel's history as they are focused on faithfulness to God and righteous leadership. The Bible keeps on calling on people to renew their relationship with God by reminding them that God's commitments are everlasting. Chronicles provides a novel perspective on the Israelites' battling experiences and their hopes, setting them up for spiritual contemplation and strengthening their faith in God.

Ezra

The book of Ezra, a sequel to the historical accounts from the 2nd Chronicles, focuses on the events surrounding the re-emergence of Jewish exiles from Babylon and back to Jerusalem. The priest, Ezra, becomes the leading character in the restoration plans with a primary focus on the revival of their spiritual life. The scenario is set in the time of the Persian Empire and the royal decree of King Cyrus to Jews in Babylon, which allowed them to return to their homeland. Culture-wise, Ezra emphasizes maintaining their religious identity and keeping the law of God. The rebuilding of the Temple comes to represent God's restoration of the relationship between the Children of Israel and Himself and the return to the way of worship. The book underlines the issues faced by the repatriates, such as the opposition of neighboring communities and internal conflicts.

Politically, Ezra faced complications working under the Persians. It shows the conflict between the demands of Jewish liberty and compliance with the Greek rulers, as Ezra aimed at fostering a community based on a commitment to the laws of God. The book of Ezra stands as a witness to God's faithfulness in answering prayers of restoration and redemption. The exiles' comeback is a turning point in Israel's history, ushering in the earliest phase of a fresh cycle in the nation's connection with God. Through the actions of Ezra and the other leaders, the Jewish people underwent a spiritual revival. They rekindled their faithfulness to the Covenant of God.

In summary, Ezra conveys a strong message about the hardships and dreams of the Israelites as they struggle to restore their country and strive for a better life. The story is a testament to the significance of faithfulness, perseverance, and reliance on God's mercy in hard times.

Nehemiah

The book of Nehemiah is the closure of the narrative of the restoration of the Jews after their exile to Babylon and the structure of the construction of the walls of Jerusalem, which happened under the supervision of Nehemiah. Nehemiah, the King's cupbearer in Persia, was permitted to return to Jerusalem to oversee the rebuilding project. Nehemiah indicates the importance of loyalty and faith in God during a difficult period. The reconstruction of the walls, on the other hand, symbolizes the city of Jerusalem's security and the safety of its people. Nehemiah's leadership should be highlighted as a fundamental component of successful governance and the enhancement of local leaders in the process of reducing social and economic challenges.

Politically, Nehemiah goes through the difficulties of governing under Persian dominion by making sure the expectations of the imperial government are correlated with those of the Jewish community. The biblical account portrays Nehemiah as a skilled administrator and diplomat who actively sought peace with surrounding enemies and executed reforms that focused on ending injustice and inequality. The book of Nehemiah is a chronicle of the Jewish people's steadfastness and obduracy in remaking their land and restoring their religions. The storyline is a display of the hardships and hopes of the Israelites as they strive to return Jerusalem to its former grandeur and revive their relationships with God.

In light of all these, Nehemiah reveals lessons about the problems of building a state and the significance of a visionary leader during critical times. A story like this will encourage you to keep pushing, even through the darkness, and to continue the fight for restoration that involves justice, security, and spiritual renewal. With Nehemiah's example, the book thus reveals the vital role of faith, endurance, and divine grace in bringing in lasting reforms.

Esther

The Book of Esther is set in the 5th-century Persian Empire when the Jews were scattered all over the world. It follows a brilliant story of Jews in the era. The story takes place in the capital city of Susa, where King

Xerxes rules a highly resourceful empire that extends from India to Cush. The central figures of the story are Esther, a Jewish orphan who became queen, her cousin and guardian Mordecai, and a Jewish slayer, Haman.

In the cultural aspect, Esther reveals the struggles of keeping the Judaism identity and commitment in a foreign environment. The story delves into issues of assimilation and resistance when Esther has to hide her true identity despite her participation in the court functions. Mordecai's refusal to show respect to the King's right-hand man, Haman, propels a series of events that culminate in the plot to eradicate all the Jews.

The Book of Esther revealed the processes of power and maneuvering that occurred within the Persian court. As Xerxes, the King, becomes impressed with Haman, a prominent official carrying the torch of his hatred against Mordecai and the Jews, the dangers of minority communities before the political schemes are highlighted. Esther's courage in preventing the planned massacre by Haman showed that there could be a turning point in the path of a nation's history through the daring act of one single person. Esther's book, in a way, sets the stage for the subsequent questions about what it means to be Jewish in exile, what is required for the survival of the Jewish people in the hostile environment, and how God cares about His people in troubled waters. Purim, the festival that celebrates the very same deliverance of the Jewish people and their enduring importance to the Jews, is celebrated on the 14th and 15th days of February.

In general, the Book of Esther describes a striking story of defiance, resistance, and divine presence amid challenging circumstances. This story is a universal lesson about faithfulness, strong bonds, and eliminating injustice, which are the values that the readers have always appreciated. Through the eyes of Esther and Mordecai's situation, the story encourages hope and perseverance during the period of uncertainty and oppression.

Moment Of Reflection

1. When you think about the significance of covenants, how can understanding these agreements influence your commitment to God?

2. Considering leadership roles, how might you apply or avoid aspects of the leadership styles seen in the historical kings in your areas of influence?

3. Reflecting on God's promises, how can the assurance of His commitments influence your outlook and decisions, especially during times of uncertainty?

4. Reflect on instances in your life when you felt God's presence. How can you nurture a more conscious awareness of His closeness in your daily experiences?

5. When you consider themes of obedience and disobedience, how do the characters' choices prompt self-reflection on your responses to God's guidance in various situations?

The historical books, however, identified several themes and consistently maintained a general theme that reveals God's continuous fulfillment of His promise to be with His children. The stories captured in these books were not just for historical or theological knowledge but to open the heart of every reader to God and His intentions. The Bible remains the best place to go to get the most from these stories.

Chapter 10: How the Old and New Testament Link

At this point, you already know that the Bible is one big, unified piece from the very start of Genesis until the end of Malachi. The Old Testament prepared the stage and laid the foundation for the good news that the New Testament brings. The New Testament is more figurative; it puts together everything the Old Testament has been trying to tell you. It is impossible not to see how the Holy Spirit divinely inspired the Bible, as it contains everything you need for your life. Every book from the Old to the New Testament is so beautifully interwoven. They complement each other, from the creation of Adam to the coming of Jesus, the Prophets of old to the Apostles of the early Church, etc. It is one grand tale of different dispensations whose relevance and significance transcends time, and its lessons are still very much applicable in today's world.

The Bible will only make sense by merging the Old Testament with the New Testament.
https://www.pexels.com/photo/a-person-holding-a-Bible-5199801/

One section would be incomplete without the other: having the New without the Old just wouldn't be right, and vice versa; there would be too many unfilled gaps and missing pieces. The Bible will only make sense by merging both parts; you cannot rule out one from the other. As a matter of fact, most of Jesus's teaching and that of his apostles always consisted of references from the Old Testament, and this isn't hard to figure out as modern-day Bibles come with cross-references that point from the Old Testament to the New and the other way around. Nevertheless, the unison between these two sections is bigger than this; the Bible is not just about the story told by the Old Testament, which was later brought to life by Christ in the New Testament. It tells of God's unending love, seen in His unrelenting pursuit of humanity, a pursuit of love that brought about the fulfillment of the promise of Jesus Christ as the savior of the world.

This chapter is here to help you simplify the link between the two sections of the Bible, identify similar themes, compare and contrast both themes based on their usage in the different sections, and have a better and more grounded understanding of the Bible in general.

The Link

It is necessary to understand the link between the Old Testament and the New Testament to help you lay a perspective in your Christian walk and know your place and role in the body of Christ. All through the Old Testament, only the people of Israel were regarded as God's chosen people. However, that changed with the coming of Jesus Christ in the New Testament, which brought about a reconciliation between you and God. However, walking under the New Covenant does not diminish the importance of the Old Testament, but rather, a focused look at both sections, side by side, will bring you a better understanding of your place and inheritance as a believer and a child of God. The New Testament is the fulfillment of the promise made in the Old Testament, and you can't do one without the other.

The Bible is a single story with two parts, the Old and New Testaments, both working together. They validate each other because they share a common author—God. Although different people physically wrote the Bible, they did so under the inspiration of the Holy Spirit. In 2 Peter 1:21, it's stated that holy men spoke as the Holy Spirit moved them. This emphasizes that every word in the Bible comes from divine inspiration.

Further confirming this, 2 Timothy 3:16 declares that all Scripture is given by the inspiration of God, serving various purposes. When you understand this, you will realize that God, as the divine author, had a central goal; the revelation of Christ to every Christian. Jesus Himself pointed this out in John 5:39, stating that the Scriptures testify about Him. So, even though you encounter Jesus directly in the New Testament, His presence has been there from the very beginning of the Bible. The central message all through the books has been Christ, making the Bible a cohesive revelation of God's plan for His people. Without the knowledge of the fall of man, their feeble attempts to reconcile back to God, the generation's worth of efforts made, the promise of a better way, and the anticipation of the fulfillment of that promise, the New Testament would not have as much significance as it does today. A new Christian must get to see where it all began, how one event led to another, and how it relates to them.

So, here are some core themes, events, people, and things that took place in the Old Testament that find more emphasis in the New Testament:

Exploring the Connection Between Old and New Testaments

The Old Testament and the New Testament may seem like separate books, but they are deeply connected. This section will take you through how the practices, laws, and ceremonies from the old days will help you understand the big picture of God's plan.

Old Testament Practices Fulfilled in the New Testament

Back in the time of the Old Testament, the children of Israel followed a system of offering animal sacrifices to make up for their sins and obtain a right standing with God. These sacrifices were tedious, as they required specific rules and rituals in Mosaic Law for each of them. Besides that, they still couldn't achieve a perfect goal of total cleanliness, as these sacrifices had to be made over and over again. Due to this, the New Testament was made to usher in a one-time change in the ways of achieving cleanliness and righteousness in the Old Testament. The old way of sacrificing animals finds its ultimate meaning and completion in the work of Jesus Christ. He is often called the "Lamb of God" because His sacrifice on the cross became the perfect offering that fulfills the purpose of animal sacrifices once and for all. The Bible says in Hebrews 9:11-12 that "Jesus, by his blood, secured eternal redemption" – this means forgiveness and a restored relationship with God. The very thing they tried so hard to establish and keep in the Old Testament was finally made available. For clarity, Jesus didn't come to get rid of the Old Testament rules but to fulfill them; this He explained in Matthew 5:17. His sacrifice on the cross totally replaces the need for animal sacrifices, and this is a big deal because it's a one-time sacrifice for all.

His sacrifice on the cross totally replaces the need for animal sacrifices, and this is a big deal because it's a one-time sacrifice for all.
https://www.pexels.com/photo/jesus-christ-stained-glass-46154/

The New Testament makes it clear that the sacrifice of Jesus is different from the old animal sacrifices, which only had a temporary impact and a symbol of something better to come. The sacrifice on the cross was a complete and final solution to the problem of sin. In Hebrews 10:19-20. The

The Bible, in Hebrews 10:19-20, encourages Christians to confidently approach God because of the sacrifice of Jesus. His sacrifice opens up a new way for everyone to connect with God. In summary, the Old Testament practice of sacrificing animals finds fulfillment in the person and work of Jesus. His sacrifice on the cross brings a whole new approach for people to relate to God.

Old Testament Laws Fulfilled in the New Testament

One very common thing about the Jewish customs was the many laws they had in place: morals, ceremonial, and civil. These laws were not just for show; they were the guiding force for the children of Israel back then. It was a core part of their lives. Now, when you look at the New Testament, especially through the teachings of Jesus, you find that these laws remain, but this time, they are fulfilled in a new way. Jesus didn't come to get rid of the Old Testament laws but to show their true meaning. Somehow, the people had lost their ways and misunderstood everything He had been trying to teach them all through several generations. Because of His love, He wanted people to understand the heart and spirit behind the rules, not just to follow them externally. In Matthew 5:17, Jesus says, "I have not come to abolish the Law but to fulfill it," meaning he wanted to complete the purpose of these laws. He had to show them and everyone after them the true meaning of the law.

One core example is the command to "love your neighbor" from the Old Testament. In the New Testament, Jesus takes it a step further, teaching everyone not only to love those close to them but even their enemies (Matthew 5:43-44). This shows a shift from just following rules to letting love transform your heart – a key aspect of the fulfillment of the law in the New Testament. This means rather than carrying it out robotically, you should obey these laws out of love for God and His people. God has always been about the heart rather than the deed. The state of the heart is what matters. When your heart is compelled by love, you will gladly obey every instruction, but if not, it will only seem rigid and forced.

In the Old Testament, the laws given to the Israelites were written on stone, external, and visible. However, with the coming of the New Covenant, there is the fulfillment of the promise in a different and better way: God Himself writes His laws on your heart, emphasizing a personal relationship over external regulations. This promise was mentioned in the Old Testament book of Jeremiah 31:33. The Old Testament laws find a new and clearer understanding in the New Testament. Jesus shows you the heart behind the rules, and the New Covenant brings a personal connection with God. It's not just about following external laws; it's about letting love transform you and embracing a deeper relationship with God through the teachings of Jesus, and in doing this, you will effortlessly fulfill every law.

Old Testament Ceremonies Fulfilled in the New Testament

In the Old Testament, certain practices such as circumcision, Passover, and the Sabbath held significant roles in the religious observance of the Israelites; just like their laws, this was also a core part of the Israelites. However, like their laws, it was done without the right understanding. As you transition into the New Testament, these practices take on a renewed and deeper meaning through the lens of

Christ and the Christian faith. The Old Testament showed how they were done, but the New Testament revealed why they are done: not the reason it was done in the Old Testament, but the reason why God established it in the first place.

Circumcision, once a physical covenant marking in the Old Testament, undergoes a profound spiritual transformation in the New Testament. It was well explained in Romans 2:29 when Apostle Paul emphasized that true circumcision is a matter of the heart, achieved through faith in Christ. It shifted from being just an external ritual to a Christian's spiritual reality, which symbolizes a profound internal connection with God.

Moving to the Passover, a pivotal event commemorating the Israelites' liberation from slavery in Egypt, the New Testament reveals Jesus as the ultimate fulfillment of this Old Testament ritual. Just like circumcision, its purpose was also reinvented. In 1 Corinthians 5:7, Apostle Paul, speaking again, describes Christ as the true Passover Lamb, sacrificed for the freedom of believers from spiritual bondage. This verse helps the Christian faith to find its foundation in the deliverance brought about by Jesus' sacrificial death and His resurrection. Also, the Sabbath, a day of rest and reflection in the Old Testament, experiences a transformative fulfillment in the teachings of Jesus. In Matthew 11:28-30, Jesus invites believers to find rest not just on a specific day but continuously through a relationship with Him. He emphasizes that the Sabbath is made for man and not man for the Sabbath, as stated in Mark 2:27.

This new understanding emphasizes the Sabbath's purpose, meaning that its observation extends beyond rigid observance to a relational aspect, where Christians discover peace and renewal for their souls. The teaching reveals that the Sabbath is a gift from God intended to bring restoration and spiritual rejuvenation to humanity. Therefore, in the New Testament context, the Sabbath finds its fulfillment in Jesus, who offers a perpetual and meaningful rest that goes beyond mere adherence to a specific day.

In essence, these Old Testament practices find a richer and more profound meaning in the New Testament. Circumcision becomes a spiritual transformation of the heart through faith, Passover finds fulfillment in Jesus as the liberating Lamb, and the Sabbath evolves into a continuous spiritual rest in a relationship with Christ. These transformations show the spiritual depth that Christ brings to these ancient practices, going beyond mere rituals to a meaningful and ongoing connection with God in the Christian faith. Christ is the heart and life force of the Christian walk; everything else would be mere practices without Him.

Old Testament Feast and Festivals Fulfilled in the New Testament

Another Old Testament practice that finds fulfillment and expression in the New Testament is the feasts, like the Feast of Tabernacles and the Feast of Pentecost. These practices held special meaning as celebrations of God's faithfulness and provision; nevertheless, in the New Testament, these feasts find their fulfillment in Jesus and the events surrounding His life, death, and resurrection, and also in the outpouring of the Holy Spirit. The Feast of Tabernacles, which is a remembrance of the Israelites' journey and God's presence with them in the wilderness, finds fulfillment in the New Testament through Jesus. When it says in John 1:14 that 'the Word became flesh and dwelt among us," the term "dwelt" used in that verse can be translated as "tabernacled" or "Inhabited" from the original Greek word. This means Jesus, in His life here and after, embodies God's presence among us, providing guidance, protection, and sustenance.

The Feast of Pentecost, initially a harvest celebration, gains new meaning in the New Testament with the arrival of the Holy Spirit. In Acts 2, you see the disciples experience the Holy Spirit coming upon them, which is symbolized by tongues of fire. This event, described in Acts 2:2-4, marked the beginning of the Church and empowered Christians like yourself to share the message of Christ globally.

So, these Old Testament feasts, although a reminder of God's faithfulness, are now more than that; they point to the fulfillment of His promises in Christ. Jesus is the living embodiment of the Feast of Tabernacles, providing spiritual guidance and protection. At the same time, the Feast of Pentecost, with the Holy Spirit's arrival, signifies the birth of the Church and the ongoing presence of God with His people. In essence, these feasts are not just historical rituals. They are living symbols of God's redemptive plan. In Jesus, the promises of provision, guidance, and the Holy Spirit find their complete fulfillment. As a Christian today, you are invited to celebrate not only the past events but also the present reality of God's faithfulness in your life. These feasts were just a glimpse of what was to come; now, they brightly reflect the transformative work of Jesus and the continuous presence of the Holy

Spirit in establishing and growing the Church.

The Holy Spirit's arrival signifies the birth of the Church and the ongoing presence of God with His people.

Adam: The First and Second

When you look at how Old Testament practices connect with the New Testament, it's important to see how Adam and Jesus fit into the picture. The Old Testament sacrifices and rules were like a setup for Jesus to come and fix things. Jesus Christ, often called the second Adam, was not just the second; He was the last, the perfect Adam. He sorted out the mess caused by *the first Adam's* mistakes, which He did by sacrificing himself to make things right with God. A look at yourself, through the lens of Adam and Jesus, is a clear depiction of the former man, which was the old you who died to give way for the new man. Jesus didn't just talk about following the rules; He actually lived them out perfectly. This made a big difference and shows you what it means to live a good life under God's new plan. So, seeing how Jesus handled things compared to Adam is like seeing the old problems get fixed by Jesus. This whole correlation between Adam and Jesus shows you God's plan for making things right.

Moments of Reflection

1. How does the idea of Jesus as the fulfillment of Old Testament practices impact your understanding of God's plan?

2. In what ways can you relate the shift from external compliance to internal transformation, as discussed in the context of Old and New Testament laws, to your own life?

3. How might the changes to rituals in the New Testament, like circumcision, Passover, and the Sabbath, impact the way you view daily practices in your faith life?

4. Think about the similarities between Adam and Jesus regarding redemption. How does this idea connect with your personal experiences of grace and forgiveness?

5. How do you see the concept of God's promises finding fulfillment in the events of the New Testament shaping your hope and trust in God's faithfulness?

6. How does seeing Jesus as the "Lamb of God," the ultimate sacrifice, shape your ideas about forgiveness and redemption?

7. How do God's grace, love, and restoration relate to your own experiences of spiritual growth and renewal?

The connection between the Old and New Testament is that of one entity with two parts working side by side to achieve a single goal by turning promises into fulfillment, turning shadows into reality, revealing the broken and flawed areas in humanity, and fixing what is broken through Jesus Christ. The Old Testament sets things up, and the New Testament makes everything happen. It is a beautiful song of God's grace, love, and making things right again. The Old and New Testaments reflect an image of the old you and the new you.

Conclusion

As you come to the end of this book, you must reflect on the journey so far. Whether you started with burning questions, a thirst for knowledge, or just stumbled upon this book, its aim was to make your exploration of the Bible straightforward and enjoyable. In these pages, you've encountered timeless wisdom, practical lessons, and insightful stories. It revealed to you the many treasures that could easily be lost in all those words. Now, you carry with you not just information but a newfound connection with the Bible.

Now that you've scanned through the books of the Bible from Genesis to Revelation, it's not about where to begin anymore; it's about cherishing your discoveries and building on them. There is still so much to uncover, but now more than ever, you are ready to take them all on. This book doesn't just end in a one-time read; you can refer to it whenever you need a refresher or a new perspective on certain things in the Bible. This is not the conclusion of your journey but a stepping stone to a deeper understanding of the Word of God. The adventure continues with every reflection, discussion, and personal encounter with the scriptures. May the insights gained be a source of ongoing joy and inspiration in your exploration of the profound teachings found within the Bible's sacred verses, with this book always by your side whenever you seek guidance.

If you enjoyed this book, a review on Amazon would be greatly appreciated because it would mean a lot to hear from you.

To leave a review:

1. Open your camera app.
2. Point your mobile device at the QR code.
3. The review page will appear in your web browser.

Thanks for your support!

Check out another book in the series

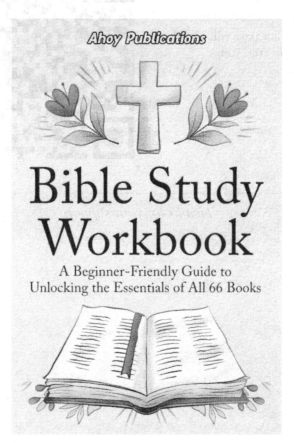

Welcome Aboard, Check Out This Limited-Time Free Bonus!

Ahoy, reader! Welcome to the Ahoy Publications family, and thanks for snagging a copy of this book! Since you've chosen to join us on this journey, we'd like to offer you something special.

Check out the link below for a FREE e-book filled with delightful facts about American History.

But that's not all - you'll also have access to our exclusive email list with even more free e-books and insider knowledge. Well, what are ye waiting for? Click the link below to join and set sail toward exciting adventures in American History.

Access your bonus here

https://ahoypublications.com/

Or, Scan the QR code!

References

Adam and Eve in the Garden of Eden - Bible Story. (2020, October 12). Bible Study Tools; Salem Web Network. https://www.Biblestudytools.com/Bible-stories/adam-and-eve-in-the-garden.html

Bible Summary - Genesis. (n.d.). Biblesummary.Info. https://Biblesummary.info/genesis

Guzik, D. (2015, June 19). Enduring Word Bible Commentary Genesis Chapter 1. Enduring Word. https://enduringword.com/Bible-commentary/genesis-1/

Duncan, L. (2001, April 1). The Third and Fourth Plagues: Gnats and Flies. Reformed Theological Seminary. https://rts.edu/resources/the-third-and-fourth-plagues-gnats-and-flies/

The Tenth Plague: the Sound of the Final Note. (n.d.). Reformedfellowship.net. https://outlook.reformedfellowship.net/sermons/the-tenth-plague-the-sound-of-the-final-note/?hilite=tenth+plague

What Was the Meaning and Purpose of the Ten Plagues of Egypt? (2013, December 31). Gotquestions.org. https://www.gotquestions.org/ten-plagues-Egypt.html

Hu, W. (2012). Unsupervised Learning of Two Bible Books: Proverbs and Psalms. Sociology Mind, 02(03), 325–334. https://doi.org/10.4236/sm.2012.23043

Mcleod, J. (2010, September 27). Wisdom in Adversity. Sermon Central. https://www.sermoncentral.com/sermons/wisdom-in-adversity-jonathan-mcleod-sermon-on-wisdom-150400

Psalms. (n.d.). Insight.org. https://insight.org/resources/ Bible/the-wisdom-books/psalms

Psalms Versus Proverbs Compare and Contrast - Free Comparison Essay Example, Compare and Contrast Paper. (2020, June 2). StudyMoose. https://studymoose.com/psalms-verses-proverbs-compare-contrast-new-essay

Turning Point. (2020, January 15). 15 Benefits to Reading Psalms and Proverbs. David Jeremiah Blog. https://davidjeremiah.blog/15-benefits-to-reading-psalms-and-proverbs/

Davisson, M. (2023, February 22). A Life-Changing Encounter for the Woman with the Issue of Blood. Cups to Crowns. https://www.cupstocrowns.com/blog/woman-with-issue-of-blood

Life of Christ - Events, Miracles, Teachings, and Purpose. (2015, April 17). NeverThirsty; Like the Master Ministries. https://www.neverthirsty.org/about-christ/life-of-christ/

The Life of Jesus: A Chronological Study. (n.d.). FaithGateway Store. https://faithgateway.com/blogs/christian-books/life-of-jesus-chronological-study

The Parable of the Sower of Seed - The Kingdom of God - Ccea - Gcse Religious Studies Revision - CCEA. (n.d.). BBC. https://www.bbc.co.uk/bitesize/guides/zd76rj6/revision/2

Understanding the Good Samaritan Parable. (2023, December 27). Biblical Archaeology Society. https://www.biblicalarchaeology.org/daily/archaeology-today/archaeologists-biblical-scholars-works/understanding-the-good-samaritan-parable/

What Is the Meaning of the Story of the Woman with the Issue of Blood? (2013, September 4). Gotquestions.org. https://www.gotquestions.org/woman-issue-blood.html

Aaron. (2017, February 22). Acts 10: Understanding the Meaning of Peter's Vision –. Path of Obedience. https://www.pathofobedience.com/scripture/acts/understanding-peters-vision/

Anderson, D. (2015, November 13). What Acts Teaches Us about Advancing the Gospel. Open the Bible. https://opentheBible.org/article/what-acts-teaches-us-about-advancing-the-gospel/

Carter, E. (n.d.). Acts: Lessons from the Early Church. Fervr.net. https://fervr.net/Bible/acts-lessons-from-the-early-church

Ministries, R. (2024, February 22). Daily Devotional Library —. Today's Daily Devotional. https://todaydevotional.com/daily-devotional-library

Study 7 The Meaning of Pentecost. (2013, April 6). Words of Life Ministries CIO. https://www.wordsoflife.co.uk/ Bible-studies/study-7-the-meaning-of-pentecost/

Introduction to Colossians. (n.d.). ESV Bible. https://www.esv.org/resources/esv-global-study- Bible/introduction-to-colossians/

Ma, C. (2021, May 18). What is The Book of Romans About? Alabaster Co. https://www.alabasterco.com/blogs/education/what-is-the-book-of-romans-about

Willems, K. (2017, April 8). Who was the Apostle Paul? - a Brief Biography (what he did and wrote) —. Kurt Willems. https://www.kurtwillems.com/blog/apostle-paul-brief-biography

Ephesus - The Loveless Church. (n.d.). Lineage Journey. https://lineagejourney.com/read/ephesus-the-loveless-church/

Guthrie, N. (2022, May 11). 10 Things You Should Know about the Book of Revelation. Crossway. https://www.crossway.org/articles/10-things-you-should-know-about-the-book-of-revelation/

Hall, E. (1992). Revelation. Journal for the Study of the New Testament, 15, 125–125. https://doi.org/10.1177/0142064x9201504814

Laodicea — The Lukewarm Church Is Neither Hot nor Cold. (2020, August 23). NeverThirsty; Like the Master Ministries. https://www.neverthirsty.org/ Bible-studies/evaluating-health-your-church/the-lukewarm-church-is-neither-hot-nor-cold/

Pergamos: The Compromised Church. (n.d.). Lineage Journey. https://lineagejourney.com/read/pergamos-the-compromised-church/

Revelation, Apocalypse, John, Patmos, Nero, Domitian. (n.d.). Ccel.org. https://www.ccel.org/ Bible/phillips/CPn27Revelation.htm

Townsend, A., Doubiago, S., Laux, D., & Scates, M. (1991). Books of Revelation. 8, 34. https://doi.org/10.2307/4021065

What does Revelation 1:20 Mean? (n.d.). Bibleref.com.

https://www.Bibleref.com/Revelation/1/Revelation-1-20.html

(N.d.). Godversusreligion.com. https://godversusreligion.com/the-letter-to-the-corrupt-church-in-thyatira-revelation/

az Bible.com. (n.d.). List of Bible Prophets. Az Bible.com. https://www.az Bible.com/prophets-in-the- Bible.html

Kranz, J. (2019, October 3). The Beginner's Guide to the Prophets in the Bible.Overview Bible. https://overviewBible.com/prophets/

Talk, F. (2023, November 15). The Prophets of the Old Testament. Hopelify Media - Share The Good News. Christian. Hopeful. Relevant. https://hopelify.org/the-prophets-of-the-old-testament/

Theology of Work. (2012, September 29). Introduction to the Prophets. Theology of Work. https://www.theologyofwork.org/old-testament/introduction-to-the-prophets/

Fairchild, M. (2011, January 28). Historical Books. Learn Religions. https://www.learnreligions.com/historical-books-of-the- Bible-700269

Howard, D. M. (2022, December 21). Introduction to the Old Testament Historical Books. The Gospel Coalition. https://www.thegospelcoalition.org/essay/historical-books/

IF:Gathering. (2021, April 26). IF:Gathering. https://www.ifgathering.com/ifequip/studies/how-to-read-your- Bible/the-historical-books-of-the-old-testament/

The Historical Books in the Old Testament. (2021, January 1). Churchofjesuschrist.org. https://www.churchofjesuschrist.org/study/manual/come-follow-me-for-individuals-and-families-old-testament-2022/22-thoughts?lang=eng

The Old Testament Historical Books (Joshua through Esther): An outline. (n.d.). Bible.org. https://Bible.org/series/old-testament-historical-books-joshua-through-esther-outline

Connecting the Old & New Testament —. (n.d.). The Chara Project. https://www.thecharaproject.com/old-and-new-testament

Old and New Testament Connection. (n.d.). Bibleone.net. http:// Bibleone.net/Old-and-New-Testament-Connection.htm

Schrock, D. (2020, September 10). The Relation of the Old and New Testaments. The Gospel Coalition. https://www.thegospelcoalition.org/essay/the-relation-of-the-old-and-new-testaments/

Theology of Work. (2013, December 6). Discovering a Link between the Old and New Testaments. Theology of Work. https://www.theologyofwork.org/the-high-calling/discovering-link-between-old-and-new-testaments/